Praise for *Crazy Happy*

"There is a power that comes when you learn that just because you don't feel something doesn't mean it's not there. Not every day feels crazy happy or truly beautiful, but in this book, Daniel brings an incredible perspective shift that will open your eyes and realign your steps to see and walk in the truth that your life, the way God sees it, is truly beautiful. If you're looking for some jaws of life to pull you out of your regularly scheduled programming and into abundance, this book is for you."

—LEVI AND JENNIE LUSKO, lead pastors of
Fresh Life Church and authors of *I Declare War*
and *The Fight to Flourish*

"It's no surprise, but Jesus regularly taught about the beautiful, happy life. In fact, he was quite bold and persistent about it. Yet in a world full of so much pain and despair, it's quite easy to lose perspective and forget his words. Daniel does a great job in this encouraging, fast-paced, and biblically centered book to remind us of Jesus's most famous words, Paul's important teachings, and God's magnificent outline for a beautiful, happy, and fulfilling life. I think you'll be blessed to read this book."

—LUIS PALAU, evangelist

"*Crazy Happy* is ultimately a recipe book. It contains the ingredients for the abundant life Jesus desires for his people. Unpacking the Beatitudes, Daniel dishes out a literary meal that is both beautiful and practical. If you want the unshakable happiness Jesus has for you, this book can show you the way."

—TIM TIMBERLAKE, lead pastor of Celebration Church, Jacksonville, and author of *Abandon*

"We all want to be happy and have fulfilling lives. But we get stuck on how to achieve that. With wit and warmth, Daniel Fusco unpacks the connection between Jesus's Sermon on the Mount and Paul's fruit of the Spirit to lead us to understand how we can be truly happy."

—ROMA DOWNEY, Emmy-nominated actress, producer, and *New York Times* bestselling author

"Daniel Fusco has been a friend of ours for years, and we are some of his biggest fans as well! Daniel's life embodies the message of *Crazy Happy*—he lives in the beautiful and joy-filled way he describes here. This is a book that is sure to bless you!"

—JEREMY (Grammy-nominated singer and songwriter) AND ADRIENNE CAMP, authors of *In Unison*

"Daniel's storytelling draws us into the greatest sources of joy in this life—and their ties to ancient Scripture—in the most beautiful ways."

—CAREY NIEUWHOF, bestselling author, podcaster, and speaker

"My friend Daniel brings the Bible to life once again to show the deep meaning that can come from pursuing something greater than ourselves. If you have been in pursuit of happiness, now is the time to discover these powerful New Testament principles."

—BISHOP DALE C. BRONNER, founder and senior pastor of Word of Faith Family Worship Cathedral, Atlanta

"In a world focused on attaining happiness, *Crazy Happy* reveals a more fulfilling and abundant source of joy that lasts a lifetime. Daniel directs our attention to the internal life change that brings rewarding joy. No one lives out the pages of this book more than Daniel."

—ROBBY GALLATY, senior pastor of Long Hollow Baptist Church, Hendersonville, and author of *Recovered* and *Replicate*

"*Crazy Happy* delivers a beautiful and biblical pathway to a happiness beyond imagination. This inspiring read flows out of the life of a man who not only lives the message but also helps us understand the attitude and actions that bring lasting genuine joy. Read this encouraging book and begin experiencing what God promises to all who desire to live a happy life."

—DR. JACK GRAHAM, pastor of Prestonwood Baptist Church

"Daniel Fusco offers a fresh look at the true happiness of the blessed life Jesus spoke of in his famous Sermon on the Mount. If you want to understand what real happiness is—and where it comes from—I recommend this book. It will take you on a journey too many Jesus followers never fully experience."

—LARRY OSBORNE, pastor of North Coast Church and author of *Thriving in Babylon*

"Daniel Fusco is one of the great teachers of the Bible today. In *Crazy Happy,* he will show you how God's gift of crazy happiness is based not on what you need to do but simply on who you are in Christ. Beautifully profound, necessary reading."

—MATT BROWN, evangelist, author of *Truth Plus Love,* and host of *Think Eternity with Matt Brown*

"*Crazy. Happy.* These are two words that equally describe Daniel Fusco! So jump on this journey to explore and unpack the Scriptures in this fresh, practical, and timely book. *Crazy Happy* is a needed reminder and road map for living and leading like Jesus."

—BRAD LOMENICK, founder of Blinc and author of *H3 Leadership* and *The Catalyst Leader*

"Daniel Fusco reminds us that when we learn to rest in who we are instead of in what we do, we find deep, long-lasting happiness. Daniel's joy and humility illuminate our journey together toward all that God has for his people."

—GREG LAURIE, senior pastor of Harvest Christian Fellowship

"Daniel Fusco lives and breathes happiness like no one else. With all the tension, anxiety, and depression in the world today, this message is so needed. Get ready to be uniquely encouraged and biblically inspired to a new level of joy."

—GRANT SKELDON, executive director of Initiative Network and author of *The Passion Generation*

"If I had two words to describe my good friend Daniel Fusco, they would be *crazy happy*. He didn't just pen the words; he lives the life. To correlate the Beatitude teachings of Jesus with the fruit of the Spirit is something I've never seen done before, and Daniel does it masterfully. Do yourself a favor and read every page, and then pass it on to all your friends. *Crazy Happy* is the book our generation needs."

—BEN COURSON, author, senior pastor of Applegate Christian Fellowship, and founder of Hope Generation

Crazy
HAPPY

Crazy HAPPY

Nine Surprising Ways to Live the Truly Beautiful Life

DANIEL FUSCO

with Lindsey Ponder

WATERBROOK

Published in the United States by WaterBrook, an imprint of Random House, a division of Penguin Random House LLC.

WATERBROOK® and its deer colophon are registered trademarks of Penguin Random House LLC.

Library of Congress Cataloging-in-Publication Data
Names: Fusco, Daniel, author. | Ponder, Lindsey, author.
Title: Crazy happy : nine surprising ways to live the truly beautiful life / Daniel Fusco with Lindsey Ponder.
Description: First edition. | New York, New York : WaterBrook, 2020.
Identifiers: LCCN 2020006516 (print) | LCCN 2020006517 (ebook) | ISBN 9780593192665 (hardcover) | ISBN 9780593192672 (ebook)
Subjects: LCSH: Happiness—Religious aspects—Christianity. | Life—Religious aspects—Christianity. | Beatitudes—Criticism, interpretation, etc. | Fruit of the Spirit.
Classification: LCC BV4647.J68 F97 2020 (print) | LCC BV4647.J68 (ebook) | DDC 248.4—dc23
LC record available at https://lccn.loc.gov/2020006516

Printed in the United States of America on acid-free paper

waterbrookmultnomah.com

9 8 7 6 5 4 3 2 1

First Edition

Interior book design by Diane Hobbing

SPECIAL SALES
Most WaterBrook books are available at special quantity discounts when purchased in bulk by corporations, organizations, and special-interest groups. Custom imprinting or excerpting can also be done to fit special needs. For information, please email specialmarketscms@penguinrandomhouse.com.

To my dearest Lynn: our life continues to be unexpected and beautiful—thank you for all of it.

To Obadiah, Maranatha, and Annabelle: the best is yet to come, so keep abiding in Jesus.

To those of you who yearn to live beautifully: let's travel this path and together learn what it means to be crazy happy.

Foreword

"What would it take to make you happy?"

That question was once asked of fifty-two thousand Americans by *Psychology Today*. Some of the most common answers included having a good job, having friends, being in love, finding recognition and success, gaining financial security, owning a house, being attractive, or being in a relationship.

What's interesting about all these attempts to find happiness is that each one is an *external* circumstance instead of an *internal* choice.

Today's popular idea of happiness is all about having the right circumstances. But God's way to happiness is about having the right attitude.

Of all the subjects Jesus could have chosen to teach about first when he began his famous Sermon on the Mount, he chose the subject of how to be happy. Why? Because he knew that everybody wants to be happy but very few people experience true, lasting happiness.

Now, when you read the Beatitudes of Jesus, they are definitely countercultural. They even *sound* contradictory: "Happy are the poor in spirit . . . Happy are those who mourn . . . Happy are the meek . . . Happy are the hungry . . . Happy are the persecuted . . ." (As Daniel will explain, "blessed" can also be translated "happy.") What? Did I hear Jesus correctly? Are you kidding?

These seem upside down and don't sound like happy to me. But Jesus was pointing out that God's way to happiness is very different than ours. It is possible to be happy, even in the worst circumstances.

If your happiness depends on your having all your problems solved first or everything in your life going perfectly, then you'll never be happy—because this world is broken. Happiness is a choice. And happiness is a habit.

Jesus is crystal clear: happiness depends on choosing the right values, the right priorities, and the right attitudes. It's not a matter of what is happening *around* you but rather what's happening *inside* you. That's why both the Beatitudes and the fruit of the Spirit are not merely a prescription for happiness—they are the pathway to spiritual and emotional health.

My good friend Daniel Fusco knows this well. He *embodies* the message in this book. Daniel is one of the most contagiously happy people I know! If you knew him, you'd love him. So read this book carefully and learn. Don't just skim through this book quickly. Savor it and discuss it with a friend. Your personal happiness is at stake.

As I write these words, the world is engulfed in anxiety over the global COVID-19 virus pandemic. Right now, many of us are being told to stay at home. I just wish everyone had this book to read while they are being quarantined. It will lift your spirits!

Rick Warren
Pastor, Saddleback Church
Author, The Purpose Driven Life

Contents

Crazy
HAPPY

Let's Get Crazy Happy

I want to ask you a big question. But first I want to give you a moment to get ready. Don't worry. This isn't a hard question. It isn't overly personal either. But it is an important question. And you don't want to overthink the answer.

Are you ready?

Take a moment. Breathe in. Breathe out.

Here it is: What is the happiest moment you can remember?

You got it? What is it?

I bet it's amazing.

My answer is simple: my wedding. It was absolutely over-the-top beautiful.

Now, I'm not saying that to score some extra brownie points with my bride, Lynn.[1] Seriously, my wedding was beautiful. To this day, it was one of my happiest moments.

---

[1] Although if you're married, you know you never can have too many of those. Brownie points are earned by the drop and spent in buckets. If you're not married, make a mental note: brownie points are always good!

We got married in Yosemite—in an Ansel Adams photograph. You know the kind I'm talking about: black-and-white film stills of the Sierra Nevada backcountry, windswept and rugged, with no one but the mule deer and bighorn sheep for company.

As a guy who grew up in New Jersey, I was blown away by the beauty of Yosemite National Park the first time I went there. I was on a road trip with a few buddies I grew up with, and we were checking out the national parks in California, southern Utah, and Arizona. But Yosemite was absolutely insane. As I looked around, I couldn't speak. I was used to the "awe" of being surrounded by huge buildings and millions of people, but now I was standing in the middle of the most majestic, awe-inspiring place I'd ever seen. I found myself just spinning in a circle, my eyes glued to the crags and bluffs towering above me. If you've never been there, I hope you can visit it sometime. Words can't really describe it.

Picture this: almost 95 percent of the park—around 750,000 acres of land—is wild and mountainous, some of the most untouched wilderness we've got left in the United States. I wasn't kidding about the photo. Ansel Adams was captivated by Yosemite, which is why I'm sure you've probably seen the park in photos at some point, even if you've never been there.

But the park is only the beginning of this story. Lynn always wanted to get married in Yosemite. During her childhood, she and her family would often visit this wonderful spot. It was one of her father and mother's favorite places, and it became even more special to Lynn when her mom passed away after a battle with cancer.

When Lynn and I got serious enough to talk about marriage, we decided we wanted to get married at the Yosemite Valley Chapel. The chapel was originally built back in 1879, and it has that kind of old-mountain-chapel quality that hits you in all the right ways when you see it. It's located in the crook of the valley, and when you look around, you realize you are literally ringed on all sides by cliffs bigger than anything you've ever seen, pockets of meadows, and (as if that weren't breathtaking enough) an incredible view of Yosemite Falls.

What could be more beautiful, romantic, and memorable than getting married in such a stunning spot *and* on the first day of spring? Lynn and I couldn't think of anything we'd like better. So imagine our excitement when we called the park service and a ranger told us the chapel was available for that date! We couldn't believe our luck.

But then we were told, "Well, given the time of year and our elevation, you've got a fifty-fifty chance of getting snowed out, and you might not be able to make it into the park to get married. And, oh yeah, if that happens, you still need to pay us for the rental even though you won't be able to get married that day."

Not exactly what Lynn and I were hoping to hear. It was a total bummer.

But if you know me at all,[2] you can guess what we did. We said, "If God wants it to happen, it'll happen! Let's just go ahead and plan it and pray that the park is open." And you probably have an idea how things went down.

We got snowed out.

---

[2] I realize that some of you might not know me, so here's a description: tall, dark, and handsome. (Well, at least the middle one. But I *have* been told I have great hair.)

No, we didn't get snowed out! You stinkers.[3]

For the weeks leading up to our wedding, the weather was perfect. On the day that we got married, it was the most beautiful day we could hope for! It was seventy-five degrees, with just a few wispy Bob Ross clouds in the sky. Purple wildflowers punctuated every stretch of green surrounding the chapel. And there was a single lingering pile of snow right in front, so all our little cousins and nephews could throw snowballs at each other.[4] I'm not kidding when I say it was the ultimate wedding.

But there was only one problem: at the start of the ceremony, my bride was nowhere to be found.

You're probably wondering, *You went through all that, only to show up and she wasn't there?* Now, Lynn is notoriously on time, but sure enough, we were supposed to get married at 10:00 in the morning, and at 10:05 she wasn't there. Then 10:10 hit—she wasn't there. And at 10:15—still not there. In Yosemite, you don't have cell reception, so I had no clue what was going on. Yeah, I was feeling a little uneasy. At about 10:20, the chapel attendant turned to me and said nervously, "Maybe she's not going to show up."

That was about all I could handle. I love Jesus, okay? And I'm a pastor. But I almost hit that attendant! Not because I was mad at him but because, geez, maybe she actually *wasn't* going to show up. And that would be the end of the world as I knew it.

---

[3] By the way, I truly don't know how you smell. But I'm sure it's . . . never mind. In case you haven't realized it yet, we are going to have fun in the footnotes. What's a book without fun footnotes?

[4] Confession: I threw a few snowballs at some specific family members.

Inside the chapel where I was waiting for Lynn, I didn't have the full picture. What I didn't realize was that because of the beautiful weather and because it was a Saturday, there was a long line of cars trying to get into the park. So my wife, who's normally right on time, was sitting at the end of that line, late for her wedding day.

Thankfully, Lynn's brother, Paul, was her driver, and Paul has absolutely no issues with speaking his mind and creating a scene. I love him for that. So when he realized how late they were, he decided to get out of the car and shout, "I got the bride in here, and she's late for her wedding day!" And everyone immediately pulled over and let them drive by.[5]

When she finally showed up—about thirty-five minutes late—my whole body sagged with relief. Whew!

As the chapel doors opened, all I saw was sunlight at first. Then I saw this beautiful silhouette of my bride in her wedding gown. Of course, I'm all Italian, so I got choked up. It took everything I had to pull it together fast. I didn't want to have bad wedding pictures because I was ugly crying before she even walked through the doors of that cute little chapel.

When I think of the happiest moment in my life, I think of that day. Was everything perfect? No. But the crazy journey it took to reach the point where Lynn and I got married made that moment all the sweeter. The beauty of that moment as I caught my first glimpse of my bride was amplified by the fact that I hadn't been sure we'd even get in the park or that she was going to show up.

---

[5]   You gotta love Californians for listening like that. Where I came from in Jersey, they wouldn't even say "fuhgeddaboudit." They'd just shake their heads no and ignore you. Those are my people.

Learning to See

Part of what makes things beautiful to us are the surrounding circumstances. I think of a famous story in the Bible—the one in which the men who followed Jesus, his disciples, were traveling on the road to Emmaus.[6] They were leaving Jerusalem, totally dejected. Bummed out doesn't even begin to describe how they felt. They thought that Jesus was the promised Messiah and Savior, so they had put all their eggs in that basket, and then he up and died. The disciples who chose to stay in Jerusalem were hiding out, fearing they were going to be next.

When I put myself in their shoes,[7] I'm guessing they thought, *All our hope was in this guy, Jesus, and what he was going to do, and now he's gone.* Like me in the wedding chapel, they just didn't know the rest of the story. On that Saturday following Jesus's crucifixion, the disciples didn't realize the cross was going to give way to an empty tomb. Although Friday was brutal, there was a resurrection coming on Sunday.

I bet you know how that feels. I know I sure do. Our lives are full of those "Saturday moments," aren't they? I can't tell you the number of times I've felt so lost in the middle of my circumstances that I haven't been able to see any beauty.

We're hitting on something fundamental to our human experience.

What I've discovered is this: plain and simple, the only

---

[6]   Luke 24:13–35.

[7]   To be more specific, in their sandals. And you *know* they'd be jealous of my Birkenstocks.

reason you and I are so dissatisfied with our lives is because we don't see them as beautiful. You think I'm making this up, but I'm not. Not seeing our lives as beautiful holds us back from the happiness and satisfaction we're meant to experience.

> Plain and simple, the only reason you and I are so dissatisfied with our lives is because we don't see them as beautiful.

I learned this in the great philosophy classroom of the college party. (Bear with me. It's worth it.) Party after party did nothing to satisfy my thirst for happiness and meaning in life. I was the guy who handled vibe control for parties all over the city. I made sure they were the *best* anyone ever went to. But I remember sitting on my dorm bed one night, saying, "This is supposed to be fun, but it's not fun anymore."

No amount of drinking or drugs made me happy. No number of relationships made me feel loved. Later, after I became a Christian, I still fruitlessly pursued satisfaction— but as a self-righteous legalist. I tried to find happiness through all the ways my life was pleasing to God—how much better I was in God's eyes than I used to be, not to mention how much better I was than other people. But none of it worked. It was all just a bandage for a deeper wound.

I've since learned that's just the normal trial-and-error process we all go through when our lives lack beauty.

True beauty is actually what we're all longing for.

You see, longing is human. And seeking satisfaction for our deep desires, even more so. But what most of us don't realize is that true beauty is actually what we're all longing for.

The famous author Fyodor Dostoyevsky said it simply: "Beauty will save the world."[8] And I believe that! But what I would argue is that beauty has *already* saved the world, and the work God wants to do today in this generation is teach us how to live the beautiful lives he designed us for—to live so inseparably linked to Jesus (the only person whose life has ever been characterized by perfect beauty) that we start to exhibit the very beauty we're all deeply longing for.

And that's also when the world around us becomes beautiful in the way God intended.

You know you have found what you are looking for when you are happy. And not just happy in the general sense, but something beyond happiness.

Our deep ache for this beyond-happy life is something we can hardly put into words most of the time. The concept of a beautiful life can be vague. We don't want beauty in an abstract sense, floating out there in the ether, something intangible that we appreciate but can't quite grasp. We want to be united with the beauty we see, to pass into it, to receive it into ourselves, to bathe in it and become part of it. As we

---

[8] Fyodor Dostoyevsky, *The Idiot* (Hertfordshire, England: Wordsworth, 1996), 492.

behold Jesus and the beauty of what God has done for us, we don't just see it from a distance; we find ourselves yearning for true oneness with Jesus.

Everyone is on a unique step of his or her journey. Some of us arrived here with serious issues, questions, and doubts about Jesus, while others of us have been following Jesus with great excitement. No matter what our personal view of Jesus is, he is still the most important and controversial person in the history of humanity. Everything he said and did matters.

We are all on this journey together, so I don't want you to be scared away if you're unsure about Jesus. It is my hope to honor the step that you are on in your journey. And if you're already following Jesus, I promise to honor your step as well.[9]

Our human love of beauty is an echoing cry in all our souls. We want to experience something beautiful not just in the world around us, not just in what we do, but in who we are. It's part of our deep longing for significance, meaning, and purpose that transcends the details of our lives and connects us to something greater. And we've all felt it.

> True beauty works itself out in our lives only as we are made one with Jesus.

---

[9]   If you are unsure about Jesus, I am truly humbled and honored that you would read this book. The same is true for those of you who already know him. Either way, we all have questions, and that's okay. Jesus is not afraid of your questions, and neither am I.

Now, I realize I just used a bunch of different terms almost interchangeably: "true beauty," "a beautiful life," "oneness with Jesus." Here's why: true beauty works itself out in our lives only as we are made one with Jesus, because only he can breathe beauty back into the deepest parts of who we are. And when this happens, we experience happiness.

Happiness Doesn't Just Happen

If Jesus is in the business of making us more like himself (aka more truly beautiful), what's our part to play? Few things in life just *happen* to us, right? So what can we do to usher in this beauty Jesus has for us?

In one of his most famous teachings, called the Beatitudes, Jesus described what it looks like to live into the beautiful life he's unrolling within us. He shared his heart on the distinctive qualities that really should just be part of who his followers are.

> # Jesus is interested in a beautiful life that defines who his followers *are*, not just what they *do*.

This is going to be key as you read the rest of this book: Jesus is interested in a beautiful life that defines who his followers *are*, not just what they *do*.

Let's take a look:

> Blessed are the poor in spirit,
> For theirs is the kingdom of heaven.

Blessed are those who mourn,
For they shall be comforted.
Blessed are the meek,
For they shall inherit the earth.
Blessed are those who hunger and thirst for righteous-
    ness,
For they shall be filled.
Blessed are the merciful,
For they shall obtain mercy.
Blessed are the pure in heart,
For they shall see God.
Blessed are the peacemakers,
For they shall be called sons of God.
Blessed are those who are persecuted for righteous-
    ness' sake,
For theirs is the kingdom of heaven.

Blessed are you when they revile and persecute
you, and say all kinds of evil against you falsely
for My sake. Rejoice and be exceedingly glad, for
great is your reward in heaven, for so they persecuted the prophets who were before you.[10]

I get it. When you read this list, almost all the characteristics that are described here are not things we would necessarily see as beautiful.

We're talking about things like poverty of spirit, mourning, meekness, hungering and thirsting for righteousness,
mercy, purity of heart, peacemaking, and persecution.

---

[10] Matthew 5:3–12.

Maybe some of those you might grab on to, but what we learn right away is that the life Jesus says is "blessed" is beautiful because this teaching of Jesus is a declaration not of what we're supposed to *do* but of who we're supposed to *be*.

After all, they're called the Beatitudes, not the Do-attitudes.[11] But isn't it hard to differentiate between the two sometimes?

In the world we live in, so many of us think that who we are is defined by what we do.

But in the Beatitudes, Jesus tells us who we already are if we are born again. If you've put your faith and trust in Jesus, the blessed person is who you are in Christ.

> In the world we live in, so many of us think that who we are is defined by what we do.

Now, I want to point out an important detail from these verses. Every one of the characteristics Jesus showcases in the Beatitudes starts with the word *blessed*. In the original Greek language, the word for "blessed" is *makarios*, which literally means somebody who has been blessed by God and is fortunate or happy.

What I find fascinating about that is Jesus links the idea of happiness with blessing and the life he intends for us to live. Often, we don't like the word *happy* because happiness

---

[11] I've heard this before, and I don't know who coined it, but it's brilliant!

has been devalued by our culture. People use that word to talk about feelings of situational well-being, feelings of circumstantial joy—such as, "The Amazon delivery guy just stopped by my house and dropped off a package, and it made me happy." So the problem with the word *happy* and the way we use it today is that everyone wants to be happy, but we think of happiness as a fleeting thought. We associate happiness with societal issues such as consumerism, self-obsession, and faithlessness, so it doesn't have much weight anymore. Like, "Hey, I'm not happy, so maybe I'll trade in my wife and kids and start a new family."[12]

But Jesus is going way deeper than that. (He usually does.)

He's saying that true happiness comes from being blessed by God.

Eugene Peterson, in *The Message* translation, originally wanted to use the word *lucky* instead of *blessed*.[13] I know you may be thinking, *I don't believe in luck because I believe in God.* But the idea of being lucky here is the idea that you got something you didn't deserve and you feel lucky you got it.

Think about it this way: if you were at the gas station[14] and decided on a whim to buy a lottery ticket and you won, you'd say, "Man, I'm lucky!" It's just an expression that

---

[12] Personally, I have no problem with people wanting to be happy. Think of the alternative. If a person said he wanted to be unhappy, I'd be heartbroken for him.

[13] Eugene Peterson, "Eugene Peterson: Translating the Beatitudes," December 19, 2017, YouTube video, www.youtube.com/watch?v=b80KhqMeM2A.

[14] When I was in high school, I worked at a gas station. It was a blast, except when it was freezing in the wintertime. Then it was awful.

means you suddenly became fortunate. Basically, the idea that Jesus gives us of blessedness being a form of "holy luck" is actually quite profound. He makes it clear the blessedness he's describing is not something you've worked to receive; it's something you've been given as a gift, not because you deserved it. Jesus gave it to you because he loves you that much.[15]

When we understand this, we discover that true happiness is not just enjoying our circumstances; it's realizing we have been blessed by God. The life he has bestowed on us was not something we deserved, but he chose to give it to us anyway.

The true happy life comes when we live within these blessings.

Future Hope, Present Blessings

We have this idea that the benefits of Christianity come to us in the future, after we die. And they do. But we also get to live out the blessings that come with following Jesus in the present. Right here and now. You're blessed *presently*.

But don't miss that Jesus said we are blessed (happy, lucky) in some crazy situations. Remember the list? Poor in spirit, mourning, persecutions, and the like. That's why I call this kind of happiness "crazy happy." Jesus is giving us the gift of happiness in the most unexpected ways *and* places. He is inviting us to find happiness in all the situations we would much rather avoid.

A quick note on the word *crazy*. Please hear my heart. In no way am I trying to minimize mental health issues. That

---

[15] I get it. "Jesus loves you" is cliché. But it is still true. His love is extravagant and extraordinary.

word has been used in inappropriate and even cruel ways. I also realize some people do not appreciate the use of ambiguous or potentially negative adjectives for the things of God.[16]

But I am not one of those people! I *love* provocative words. Plus, I realize that younger generations love to use language in these ways.[17] So I am using the word *crazy* with its most positive contemporary connotation: intensely enthusiastic and passionately excited,[18] with a little bit of irrationality thrown in for good measure. Crazy happy is the life Jesus has for us.

Oftentimes when I hear someone teach the Beatitudes, they are described as a chain of imperatives—things Jesus commands us to do. But another interesting thing we learn from the Greek here is that the mood of what Jesus is sharing in the Beatitudes is in the indicative tense, which literally means it's a statement of fact. That's what I mean when I say the Beatitudes tell us who we are, not what we have to do. It doesn't mean that now we have this responsibility to act a certain way; it means that because we are given this life in Jesus, we get to live blessed lives when we understand who we truly are in him. This is the crazy happy life.

That's why James said faith without works is dead.[19] You

---

[16] Like the worship song that speaks of the "reckless" love of God. Some people do not appreciate calling God's love reckless, as some definitions of *reckless* have negative connotations.

[17] Like calling something "good" or "sick." Or my son Obadiah's favorite: calling "fun" "savage"!

[18] Dictionary.com, s.v. "crazy," accessed November 11, 2019, www .dictionary.com/browse/crazy.

[19] James 2:14–26.

see, faith apart from a way of changed living is not really faith at all; it's just an idea we hold in our minds. God wants us to take the next step with him when we believe. He wants what we believe to be lived out.

God is interested in theology with legs on it. He wants us to put feet on our faith and live it out into the world. It's what I call *applied theology.*

The Beatitudes show us we need to know who we are in Christ and live accordingly.

And what's truly wild about this adventure we call "faith in Jesus," as we live according to his desires for our life, is that Jesus says there's a result we can expect. It's a promise he's given us!

Again and again, he said, "Blessed are _____, for theirs is _____." That means who you are leads to an outcome. Can you imagine walking by the neighbor's house and seeing a lion caged up in the backyard with a bunch of house cats and eating dry cat food? It's a crazy thought,[20] but the point is, that lion wasn't destined for a backyard; he was destined to roam in the savannah wilderness in Africa! He was made for something so much more.

We are the same way. We are children of the Most High God, saved by the finished work of Jesus, and we are free to live that out beautifully in the world. Now, our motivation for living godly should never be to get the outcomes we want. (That's backward!) On the contrary, our motive to live as Jesus wants is to know him and love him more. And when-

---

[20] That's actually not crazy. That would be awesome. If that is you, you are totally my hero.

ever life gets hard, we can always fall back on his promises to us in the Beatitudes.

So if you want a beautiful life, put your faith and trust in Jesus. And here's a key to life as a follower of Jesus: it's not just believing in Jesus one time when you commit to him; it's about following him every day as well. It's about walking with him.

See, too many of us have this idea that when you're born, you're born and that's it. It's a great thing to be born, but what's next? If you never interact with your parents again, will you grow? It won't happen, right? And it's the same way with Jesus. You put your faith and trust in him one time. That's salvation. But then the adventure begins: you follow him every single day so that you grow.

If we want to experience the crazy happy life God intends for us in Jesus—the life that fills our longings—we have to internalize this new reality. God's ideas are unique. They're so different from our culture. But they lead to exactly where you and I want to be. And better yet, they lead to what God wants for us.

His beauty changes everything. It comes as a gift, and when we live into his beauty, the world changes.

What's both interesting and heartbreaking is if you ask most people who don't go to church how they would describe the Western church, you'll likely find it doesn't go all that well. Very few people are going to list off the Beatitudes when they describe the church. Very few people are going to describe Christians as "poor in spirit," "hungering and thirsting for righteousness," "mourning."

Don't get me wrong—I *love* the church. She is the body

and bride of Christ. But if we're real with ourselves, we've got to know that the rest of society is not thinking Beatitudes when they see how we live most of the time.[21]

I would venture to say it's really urgent for us to figure out how to get back to a faith that's beautiful—for the sake of a dying world, and also because that's how Jesus loves us to live. And at the end of the day, living beautiful lives that are pleasing to Jesus is what it's all about.

But I want to add another layer to help us discover the crazy happy life.

From Crispy to Crazy Happy

At the beginning of every summer, we take some family time. Just us. After many years of marriage, Lynn and I have three great kids: Obadiah, Maranatha, and Annabelle. We pull them out of school a little bit early (we are the coolest parents!) and head to one of our favorite spots, Donner Lake. Donner Lake is next to the famous Lake Tahoe on the California-Nevada border. By the end of another school year and a full season of ministry, we always look forward to this special time to rest, clear the decks, and reset. We all need it individually and as a family.

Just a few years back, I was particularly crispy. That's the word I use when I am feeling tired, dried up, beaten down, and just plain blah. *Crispy*. I was skidding into our vacation time, I wasn't feeling all that healthy, and my proximity to vacation was what was keeping me going at that point.

---

[21] I like to say that Jesus needs new PR. Then I remind people that *we* are his PR.

I usually make some sort of plan for spiritual growth for these times. Given my crispiness, I decided that instead of seeking to consume a lot of Scripture, I would simply soak in just one passage. So I chose the Beatitudes. Day after day, it was the only thing I read, until I had the passage memorized and a journal full of thoughts and insights I picked up along the way.

After about a week, in one of my times of reflection, I had a strange thought:[22] *Aren't there the same number of beatitudes as there are fruits of the Spirit?* That's the kind of thing I randomly think of. So I quickly turned to Galatians 5:22–23.

Yep, there are nine fruits of the Spirit: love, joy, peace, longsuffering, kindness, goodness, gentleness, faithfulness, and self-control. That's nine fruits to go along with nine beatitudes. That's interesting, isn't it? I wondered if something was there.

I thought, *What would happen if I lined them up?* So in my journal, on one side of the page, I wrote out the Beatitudes, and on the other side, I wrote out the fruit of the Spirit. Because I believe the Bible is unique, inspired, and perfect, I decided the order of the words was by design, so I resisted the temptation to take the words out of order. I just let them be in the order they were written.

As I looked at the paper, I instantly realized that this is important. *Really* important.

Both the Beatitudes and the fruit of the Spirit tell us simi-

---

[22] It could have just been my ADD kicking in after trying to focus on one passage of Scripture for that long.

lar things. Both are not explanations of what we do but of *who we are*. Both explain the unique qualities of what it means to be given the gift of life in Jesus.

Think about a fruit tree. Fruit is born in its own time, simply because of the tree it stems from. Jesus said we will know a tree by its fruit. He also said God is glorified by us bearing fruit, and that is impossible unless we abide in him.

In other words, fruit can't produce itself. Its growth is a by-product of its ability to find its life from the tree itself. This is exactly what Jesus told us in John 15:4. So when you put the Beatitudes together with the fruit of the Spirit, you find that, as a pairing, they give us an absolutely stunning view of what a beautiful life is made of.

Think about the fruit of the Spirit again: love, joy, peace, longsuffering, kindness, goodness, gentleness, faithfulness, and self-control. Almost everyone agrees that this list contains qualities of a crazy happy life. But when we link these traits up with the Beatitudes, we start to learn how and where that fruit is cultivated. These nine pairings are like movements of a symphony for us to explore and soak in.

One of the greatest areas of tension for us is we all want to live happy lives, but we have a nagging feeling that our lives aren't what they could be. So we try to live better. We try to make life more beautiful. And with every attempt to cultivate more beauty, we continually find ourselves not quite there.

So the hamster wheel keeps spinning.

You might be thinking, *Fusco, it's not that hard to find beauty in life. You just need to look for it, and you'll see it all around you.* I hear you. It's been said that beauty is in the eye of the beholder. This is fundamentally true. Each of us sees beauty in different things. But God sees certain things as beautiful as well. And what he thinks becomes our road map. When we align our ideas about beauty with that of our Creator and Sustainer, true beauty emerges.

I have a sneaking suspicion you picked up this book because you want your life to be truly beautiful. You want to live crazy happy. So do I. That is also why I needed to write this book in the first place. I wanted to find the road map to a crazy happy life. I wanted to learn how to cultivate a truly beautiful life.

So let's take this journey together. Come explore these passages of Scripture and the amazing realities tucked inside. Let's put ourselves right in the middle of these passages and watch them bloom in our lives. Nine surprising and simple ways that lead to a beautiful life. A crazy happy life.

I promise to be as honest as possible. I'm traveling this path too.

Sounds beautiful, doesn't it?

Let's find out together.

2

The Crazy Happy Way of Love

Blessed are the poor in spirit,
For theirs is the kingdom of heaven.

—Matthew 5:3

The fruit of the Spirit is love.

—Galatians 5:22

Obadiah, Maranatha, and Annabelle.

Those are my three amazing kids.[1] And let me tell you, I have yet to experience another joy equal to the joy of parenting. It's absolutely amazing! Yes, it can be hard, but it's the best thing I've ever poured my heart and energy and life into.

That said, getting my kids out the door and headed to school is actually one of the most excruciating things my wife and I do on a daily basis. It's not for lack of trying. Lit-

---

[1] If my kids are reading this book, you are truly amazing. Please just make sure you clean your room, brush your teeth, and walk the dog. Love you.

erally, Lynn and I have attempted every trick in the book to work it out and make our mornings easier. But no matter what we do, "it ain't easy" (to quote David Bowie).[2]

When the alarm rings, it's the opening note in a symphony. And I'm not talking about just any symphony. This one's a multimovement symphonic arrangement that sometimes seems to have lost its conductor. There are *lots* of moving pieces, all going in different directions. In our case, we're herding two girls and a guy, so yeah, we've got bathroom management. (Will someone please write a how-to book on this already?) We have everyone's backpacks to pack, sandwiches to stack and throw into lunch boxes. We have to make sure everybody has *actually* brushed his or her teeth.[3] And don't forget; everyone has to give Mom (or Dad) a huge hug and a kiss before leaving.[4] It's hard, you know?

But once the kids are in the car and we pull out of the driveway and into our day, then, like the calm after the storm, our morning gets really fun. Believe it or not, one of Lynn's and my greatest joys as parents is driving our kids to school.

Morning car rides have become one of our favorite family prayer times. We bring our day before God and prepare ourselves for what it will hold. As part of this, one of the things I love to do with my kids is put on the whole armor of God together. Remember that passage from Ephesians 6? It's *so* good.

You might wonder what that looks like. Well, *loud,* for

---

[2] David Bowie, "It Ain't Easy," *The Rise and Fall of Ziggy Stardust and the Spiders from Mars,* 1972, RCA Records.

[3] Did anyone feed the dog?

[4] Not to mention, is everyone fully clothed?

one thing. Picture this: our kids shouting out the pieces of the armor of God, and my driving getting slightly "creative" as I try to keep an eye on the road *and* on what Annabelle's shoving in her mouth in a delayed breakfast. And over it all, we're joyfully praying.

If you're familiar with the apostle Paul's description of the armor of God, you know there are quite a few pieces involved. The people of God are encouraged to put on the helmet of salvation, the breastplate of righteousness, the belt of truth, and the gospel of peace. Besides all that, we have the shield of faith and "the sword of the Spirit, which is the word of God."[5]

So far, so good. But my kids are *my* kids, which means they're just a little cray-cray,[6] and they think a couple of pieces are missing from the armor of God—things we can add on to make it even better. So, over the years, the armor of God has expanded in my family. And you know what? I think God loves it! I remember when one of my kids asked, "Why doesn't the armor have a jet pack?" Good question. Well, now ours does: the jet pack of praise. And, of course, every good suit of armor needs a pocket too. (Or so I am told.) So there's the pocket of prayer as well.

Now, don't get mad at me about this next example, but Obadiah plays sports (some of you can see where this is going already), so he sees the importance of having an athletic supporter with the armor too. I mean, if you've played

---

[5] Ephesians 6:17.

[6] Notice I said the cray-cray part of my kids is because of me, not because of Lynn. Why? Because she is awesome. She just had a lapse in judgment when choosing a husband.

a contact sport, can you disagree?[7] So we put on "the cup of protection." I know, I know. But I actually think God's all for the cup of protection. He's our refuge, our strength—he gets it!

This armor praying began when our little Annabelle was about four. She started to lead us in this, and it was super cute. After putting on the armor, we would all pray together. I'll never forget one of those early days. Annabelle was so excited to pray and launched into a mighty one. Just one problem: we couldn't understand her. She still had that little chipmunk voice, so nobody had a clue what she was saying. I remember looking at Obadiah and mouthing, *"Bro, I have no clue what she's saying right now!"* "Me neither," Obadiah replied, "but the Lord knows, and he loves it."

Wow. Obadiah, at such a young age, really understood the heart of God. And at that moment, what struck me was the beauty of God's simplicity.

You see, at the end of the day, God wants our hearts. It's not about being big or brilliant or even intelligible. It's about being *his*—about responding to him like a kid. Although none of the rest of us in the car understood Annabelle's prayer, the Lord did.

And I think he loved it.

Simply Humble

In Matthew 18:1–5, when Jesus talked about entering the kingdom of heaven like a child, I believe he meant more than

---

[7]   I know what you're thinking, but here's my overall endorsement: just think about all the different rad gifts in life that God gives us and how cool it is to celebrate all of them! How is this any different? Change my mind. ☺

we usually think. It's more than just having childlike faith; I think he meant that kids are simple, and we need to become like that too. I don't mean kids are dumb or they can't have deep thoughts. I know the opposite is true. But there's a simpler way of seeing the world. Kids have it. Most grown-ups don't.[8]

As we get older, we become more complex. We become more self-aware, more insecure. Life spirals from there, seeming to get more complicated every day. Sooner or later, we wind up realizing that relationships seem so much harder than they used to, so much more painful.

Sometimes this "growing up" keeps us from experiencing all God has for us in Jesus. This is the drama of life.[9] It's also the problem of life. It, for good reasons or bad, becomes why it seemed so easy once (for most of us) to be crazy happy. It's why it feels so much harder now.

So our lives get complicated. But deep down, we all remember a better way. Yet what's hard to own sometimes is that our biggest source of complexity is us.

We are the most problematic participants in our lives. We complicate our relationships, our work environments, our pursuits in life. And then we try to fix the people around us,

---

[8]   You know what? Jesus loves simple. Think about the number of times you find Jesus in the Gospels caring for people who came to him in simplicity. I think of Matthew 8:2 and the leper who says, "Lord, if You are willing, You can make me clean." He understood the heart of God too—that God is both able and willing to help his children. Nothing complicated there.

[9]   In the Fusco home, we say, "Save the drama for your llama." And since we don't have a llama, we got no time for drama.

or we get extra introspective and stare inward at our own motives, hoping to simplify.

Like when we have interactions that strike us as a bit odd, and we didn't get the responses we expected. For many of us, before we know it, we are down the rabbit hole about how they must feel something negative about us. And that thing gets big in our heads really quick. We begin apologizing. Or worse, we get frustrated with them. Oftentimes, they haven't had one thought about us. They are busy thinking through their own stuff. But in our complications, we make mountains out of molehills.

Either way, our eyes get fixed on ourselves, and when we become preoccupied with ourselves, that is pride. Did you catch that? The pride that increases in our hearts as we "grow up" makes us complex.

But there's good news: the opposite is true as well. Becoming more humble means we begin to simplify.

Few of us have ever wished to be more humble. Usually when we're up to our necks in the drama of life, we want to puff ourselves up to feel better about ourselves.[10] After all, humble people don't seem to get ahead very often. Humble people are (we think) too quiet, too passive, too easy for someone bigger and louder to push aside. But, of course, that's us believing a lie. Jesus, *because* of his humility, was able to be perfectly strong.

He was strong in his simplicity. Is it any wonder that this real Jesus opened his famous sermon in the Beatitudes by reminding us of this crazy way of life? He painted a beautiful

---

[10] If you're one of the few who don't, I applaud you.

but shocking picture of what a really blessed life is, starting with how we *enter* the kingdom of heaven. With this truth, he gave us the key to cross the threshold into his kingdom. Once we're inside, there will be a whole host of other fruits that begin to cascade from our kingdom lives. (But more on that later!)

Remember that wild and unexpected blessing word *makarios*? Notice the first type of person Jesus calls blessed (*makarios*) in the Beatitudes.

Matthew 5:3 reads,

> Blessed are the poor in spirit,
> For theirs is the kingdom of heaven.[11]

What's fascinating about Jesus is that only he would start out with, "Blessed are the poor in spirit." Think about this! Let it sink in. He's saying, "Oh how lucky are the poor in spirit!" Can we all agree that nobody talks like that today? None of us feels *lucky* when being humbled, do we? Talk about crazy happy!

This is one of the primary reasons our Western society has issues with the real Jesus. Those who are poor in spirit

---

[11] To put this idea of simplicity another way, check this out: Jesus says the kingdom belongs to the poor in spirit. In Matthew 18:1–5, Jesus says only those who become like little children will enter the kingdom of heaven. Who enters the kingdom of heaven? The poor in spirit, or those who are like children? Jesus identifies two groups of people, but I want to argue that those two groups are one and the same. The common element between children and those Jesus calls "poor in spirit" is they both possess the humility and simplicity to see their own need, their own poverty, and to come to Jesus in that neediness, expecting his help. Humility is how we enter the kingdom at any age.

are by definition acknowledging their spiritual bankruptcy: they know they aren't enough. In our highly individualistic, "work hard, play hard" society, the idea of spiritual poverty flies in the face of our value sets, especially the cultural movement to value our sense of self above anything else. When we love ourselves the way culture encourages us to, we end up narcissistic and self-obsessed. Yes, under the banner of God's love for us, we should love ourselves.[12] But that love isn't a self-focus; it comes from walking in the reality that we are loved by God. Ironically, it's by taking our eyes off ourselves that we can see and value who we really are. What an incredible gift.

I don't care whether you were raised in the church, came to faith later in life, or are just exploring Jesus, or whether you're a baby boomer or a millennial (not to mention Gen X or Z)—if you grew up in Western society, you've been nurtured in an environment that says don't ever let *anybody* know that you failed. The message from all sides is: If you fail, blame someone else.[13] Or come up with a convincing reason for why what you did is actually not a failure at all. Justify yourself. Like the old deodorant commercial said, don't ever let them see you sweat. If we can't be perfect, we at least have to act like we are at all costs.

Culture Collision

Think for a minute about social media. We take a thousand selfies just to get that perfect one to post, to show everyone

---

[12] This is what I like to call the Upward, Inward, Outward framework of the Greatest Commandment.

[13] And we all can admit the blame game is as old as the Garden of Eden.

we have it all together. We're all fluffing up our virtual résumés, our online personas, all the time. It is all about appearances, and we're secretly terrified for that bubble to pop.

That's how we were nurtured. That's what our culture rewards us for. Then Jesus shows up and runs roughshod right over it. He defines the blessed, beautiful, crazy happy life differently from anyone else before or after him—defines it as humility.

What God sees as beautiful is somebody willing to say, "I bring nothing to my relationship with God except my own brokenness and sinfulness." That feels kind of depressing to acknowledge, doesn't it?

Jesus drives smack-dab, head-on into a massive collision with our culture. The famous preacher Dr. Martyn Lloyd-Jones said about being poor in spirit, "It means a complete absence of pride, a complete absence of self-assurance and of self-reliance. It means a consciousness that we are nothing in the presence of God."[14]

In his book *Mere Christianity*, C. S. Lewis put it this way:

> Do not imagine that if you meet a really humble man he will be what most people call "humble" nowadays: he will not be a sort of greasy, smarmy person, who is always telling you that, of course, he is nobody. Probably all you will think about him is that he seemed a cheerful, intelligent chap who took a real interest in what *you* said to *him*. . . .

---

[14] Dr. Martyn Lloyd-Jones, *Studies in the Sermon on the Mount* (Grand Rapids, MI: Eerdmans, 1984), 50.

If anyone would like to acquire humility, I can, I think, tell him the first step. The first step is to realise that one is proud. And a biggish step, too. At least, nothing whatever can be done before it. If you think you are not conceited, it means you are very conceited indeed.[15]

Here's my Original Fusco Translation of that:[16] humility is allowing the true and living God to divorce each one of us from our complete and total obsession with ourselves. That's the key to simplicity. And it's really good news.

Humility calls us to see things the way God sees them and see ourselves the way God sees us—that we are broken and flawed, and that we don't get everything right. And we are helpless to heal ourselves on our own. (Ouch!)

God's beauty rises up from the ashes of our humility. Then humility throws open the gates of the kingdom of God and leads us into the potential of a truly beautiful life.

When we let go of our desperation to be right, we grow in our willingness and desire to walk in what is right. When that shift in our mindset happens, now all of a sudden we begin to say, "Lord, I need you"—and really mean it.

God's beauty rises up from the ashes of our humility.

---

[15] C. S. Lewis, *Mere Christianity*, C. S. Lewis Signature Classics, rev. ed. (New York: HarperCollins, 2015), 128.

[16] That would be the OFT, for short.

That need never changes as we age. I remember that when I came to know Christ, I was struggling with drugs and promiscuity and all kinds of uncleanness, and I was really, really obnoxious.[17] And, praise God, now I'm not doing drugs, and I am joyfully and faithfully married to the best person I know. I love that all these things get cleaned up in Christ. But that doesn't mean God's finished with me. It's always a process. I still have other things to work on, and I always will.

We start to recognize the reality that he who began a good work in us *will continue* until the day of Christ Jesus[18]—so he's not done with us yet, in other words.

Humility gives us access to the kingdom of God, which is just another way of saying humility gives us access to Jesus. Without humility, we have no access to Jesus. Being proud is not just a sin. It's the *root* of sin. It's distance from our impossibly humble God.

I realize that sounds intense. I'm not saying you need to become perfectly humble at this very minute. If you're in Christ, that means you have already begun this process! Humility is one of the primary lanes you should run in. So run in it! You are already poor in spirit by the very fact that you said yes to Jesus in the first place. When you put your trust in him, you acknowledged in that moment, "I cannot save myself. I need a Savior." That is a beautiful act of humility—an enormous first step to God's crazy happy "poorness" of spirit.

---

[17] I can practically hear some of you snickering right now, and I get it. I'm still working on the obnoxious part, but hey, we're all works in progress.

[18] See Philippians 1:6.

The problem for many of us is that we fall into the same trap the Pharisees in Jesus's day did. We know God's Word. We even *like* the Word. We're seeking to follow the Word. But what we're missing is more basic. We can easily lose the simple heart of God that children grasp so easily. The Pharisees were so "religious" that they missed God's heart. They missed this beautiful, simple humility lived out in the midst of everything that was going on in their world.

All along, it was the spiritually impoverished Jesus was looking for.

They thought God wanted to see the richness of their souls. But all along, it was the spiritually impoverished Jesus was looking for.

Think about this in our celebrity culture. Jesus just hung out with the normal people—or, even worse, the criminals and reprobates of society! He was judged for it. People were like, "Dude, what's your rabbi doing, man? Why's he hanging out with *those* people?" And Jesus answered and said, "Those who are well have no need of a physician."[19]

Do you see it? Jesus is so *simple.* He had no mental checklist for who he associated with. Prostitutes and Pharisees both got to eat with him. What mattered was humility. He just said (I'm paraphrasing), "Look, I didn't come to call those who think they're righteous because of their religion. I came to call those who know they're sinners."

Times change, but people pretty much stay the same.

---

[19] Mark 2:17.

Pharisees in the church today are those who at some point gave their lives to Jesus and want to follow the Word but have lost God's heart for people. They've forgotten where they came from—or never really knew it in the first place. Instead of saying, "I need Jesus," they start to look at other people and say, "*They* need Jesus. I can't believe someone would do that."

If this is you, be careful. Whenever we find ourselves in the "I can't believe they . . ." party, we've walked away from poverty of spirit. We may be in Christ, but we're missing out on the beautiful life and sabotaging our own happiness.

We live in a day where people who don't know Jesus don't feel much love from people who do. This is a huge spiritual problem. Without the humility Jesus is looking for, we have no testimony to a dying world.

> We live in a day where people who don't know Jesus don't feel much love from people who do.

I love to engage with people who don't go to church and don't know Jesus—you know, the "real world" out there. Most of them don't love Christians so much, and they'll often tell you it's because the church is full of hypocrites. I don't disagree. (Granted, the whole world is full of hypocrites.) This is tough to hear, but it's probably no surprise to any of us. Because of this view of Christians, humility is not only the path for us to enter the kingdom of God, but it's the way in which the church can transform the wider world's poor opinion of us. It lets us become a winsome, beautiful witness to help usher a dying world into the kingdom of God.

Want proof? Look again at the life of Jesus, who even in his divine perfection lived humbly.

Those people who were considered outsiders by the religious authorities *loved* to be with Jesus, even though he didn't do all the things they were doing. In fact, he lived completely differently from how they did. Yet they felt comfortable to come to him and share their lives with him because even though he was perfect and he never did anything wrong, there was room in his heart for them.

Why? Because the fruit of humility is love.

Humility Is the Crazy Way to Authentic Love

Remember earlier when I said that we can see how God defines the beautiful life in two places in Scripture? Even though they're in different books from different authors, I think they're intimately related. The sections talk about what Jesus calls the blessed life (found in the Beatitudes) and what Paul calls a fruitful life (found in Galatians 5:22–23). When we line up the two passages, the teachings really pop. I believe that when we live in the way Jesus calls blessed, the Spirit produces fruit in our lives—the kind of qualities that make for beauty and happiness, the crazy happy way!

What we find here is that the blessed place of poverty of spirit leads us right into the fruit of the Spirit that is love. Think about it. What's the ultimate example of love the world has ever seen?[20] Jesus willingly humbled himself—he

---

[20] No, I'm not talking about *The Notebook*. But truth be told, I totally ugly cried at the end of that movie.

lived in submission to his Father, put on human flesh, and willingly laid his life down for his own creation—all because of his love for the Father and humanity.

When we live our lives always cognizant of the reality that we are sinners[21] in need of our Savior, we maintain hearts of humility, and that posture ultimately allows us to love others with the same humble love that Christ showed. It's undeniable evidence that his Spirit is in us.

This crazy idea of happiness coming from poverty of spirit leads us to think differently. The question becomes, "Why would I ever *not* love another person?" Let that question land for a second.

When we forget where we've come from, we lose the ability to meet people where they are.

Think about people you don't love right now.[22] Why don't you love them? Maybe they have hurt you and you think they don't care about others the way you do. Maybe they don't live lives that honor God. Maybe you can't fathom how they could vote the way they did. Or you can't believe they would

---

[21] It's important to remember that being sinners doesn't mean we are the worst possible versions of ourselves; it means that none of us is the best possible version of who God made us to be.

[22] I know, I know, some of you are over-the-top, super holy, and you're like, "Fusco, I love everybody." But we're all human here, so I know you at least kinda don't like everyone. So think about the people you really dislike instead.

watch that movie. Or that they would go to church only once per month. Or they would be attracted to *that* person. And the list goes on.

When we start to look at the people we struggle to love with poverty of spirit, we realize the problem isn't them; the problem is us. My problem is me. Your problem is you. The issue is in the posture of our hearts, because when we forget where we've come from, we lose the ability to meet people where they are.

Humility teaches us we're all the same, just with different life details. We might have unique issues, but the propensity to live in a way that destroys our own lives is in all of us. And if it weren't for God's grace, we'd be sitting in the exact same seat as that person whose life is in shambles. Humility frees us to walk in the crazy happy way of love.

The modern Western church is an unfortunate example of this. Although we are supposed to be the body of Christ, we are often a place of extremes when it comes to embracing people who don't follow Jesus. Both extremes are rooted in pride. On the one hand, there are those of us whose pride manifests in a pharisaical spirit. We judge and snicker or look down our noses with contempt. On the other hand, there are those of us who are so fed up with hypocrisy in the church that we've started to say, "We'll just love everybody and not worry about sin. God can take care of it," and we affirm everything.

We blame the world for not feeling loved by us. We say things like, "Well, that's their fault 'cause they think that if we don't affirm their lifestyle, we don't love them." And what I want to say is that, actually, it's *our* fault. Neither judgment nor total affirmation is love. If you really were humble and loved people, you could say, "I don't agree with you, but I still love you." And as time goes on, those relationships become places of God's light in the people's lives (and in ours), regardless of the choices they're making.

If you look at the life of Jesus, he doesn't walk around correcting people who aren't following him until they make the choice to follow him. He does correct those who claim to follow God (for instance, the disciples and the Pharisees). You'll remember how Jesus invites us to lovingly correct our brothers and sisters: "If you see a speck in your brother's eye, first you have to pull the plank out of your own eye. Then go deal with your brother's speck."[23] Jesus is stating the obvious: a speck is a piece of sawdust, and a plank is a two-by-four.[24] Rather than being like, "Bro, you got sawdust in your eye," take the plank out of your eye first. 'Cause if you don't pull the plank out, you'll knock your brother out with your issues.[25]

But here's the cool thing. When you *know* you have garbage, too, and you're willing to deal with it, then you can go and say, "Listen, I'm nobody. I got me a whole lumberyard going on in my eye. You don't even know. I got particleboard. I got two-by-fours. I got woodblock. I got some composite

---

[23] See Matthew 7:5.

[24] Okay, so if you're a carpenter, I know my technical explanation of a plank might not meet your standards, but you get the point.

[25] And don't miss that to remove a speck from someone's eye, you have to get really close to her face to see it. If you haven't removed the plank from your own eye, your attempt to help remove the speck will end up in a concussion! Do you think she'd rather have dust in her eye or a concussion? Exactly!

material. I'm pulling all kinds of junk out of my eye. But I did notice that this speck's messing you up a little bit. I'm not your judge. I'm not your jury. I just see this in you, and I care about you and don't want you to get hurt."

Isn't that totally different from when somebody comes and judges you and says all sorts of stuff about you as if his or her poop smells like roses?[26] If we humble ourselves before God and love others as they are, the goodness of the Lord through our lives can lead them to repentance. God's kindness shines out from our lives and invades theirs. And God may just transform them as he has transformed you and me. I love the phrase "Transformed people transform people."

That's what I love about the beautiful life Jesus invites us to: it spreads from our hearts to the hearts of others.

But let's be honest: none of us love to be humbled.[27] However, the Bible teaches us we'll be humbled whether we like it or not. Now, the way I look at it, it's not tough to figure out which side is best. We either humble ourselves before the hand of God and he lifts us up, or ultimately our sin will humble us. But either way, you will be humbled. It's just a matter of whether it's redemptive or not—whether we welcome it as Jesus did or fight it, kicking and screaming. And

---

[26] Gimme a break. I'm raising middle schoolers and a kindergartner, man, so I am chock-full of poop references. But if my making a poop reference is offensive, let's just call it dung, as certain versions of the Bible do.

[27] As a pastor, I always get nervous when someone asks me to pray for him or her to be humble. Mostly it's because I know that if God works in that area, the same person will soon be asking for prayer to remove the situation that is creating the humility.

the stakes are high. The world needs the church of Jesus to truly be poor in spirit in this generation because without our humility, they'll never experience God's love.

In reality, all we're doing is pushing away the very people Jesus died and rose again to redeem and killing our opportunity to tell them about Jesus.

Here's the deal: if you would not call yourself poor in spirit or humble today, you've actually left the place where Jesus meets you. He starts with humility and the beauty that comes from loving others. We're supposed to dwell forever in humble gratitude for our salvation, at the foot of the cross, and share that with everyone around us.

That's how Jesus works. When we come to him in poverty of spirit, he is faithful to bear the fruit in our lives he wants us to bear. He doesn't leave us as orphans.[28] He helps us love others in the way he's directed us to live.

But as good as this beautiful life is, this is only the beginning. Poverty of spirit is the doorway to the kingdom of heaven, where we begin to walk in love for God and humanity. But that means when love begins to take root in our hearts, we're only standing on the threshold of all the beautiful fruit God wants to unfold in our lives.

If you're ready for what's next, turn the page.

---

[28] See John 14:18.

3

The Crazy Happy Way of Joy

Blessed are those who mourn,
For they shall be comforted.
—Matthew 5:4

The fruit of the Spirit is . . . joy.
—Galatians 5:22

A number of years ago, I traveled with several friends and other pastors on a missions trip to Lima, Peru. If you've ever done cross-cultural ministry, you know it's going to be a great trip if everything goes wrong, right? It usually means God is up to something good. Well, this was one of those times.

Back then, I was one of those people who would update a Facebook account with the details of a trip, so I had been posting about heading to Peru. I took off from my home airport without a care. But when I landed in Lima, I discovered that someone had hacked my Facebook account while I was logging in on a layover. The hacker was sending messages to all my friends, asking for money 'cause I got arrested and needed to post bail! Even my bride, Lynn, got one of those messages.

In case you've wondered about this before, let me tell you, it's never a good thing when your wife gets a message informing her that you are in jail in a foreign country.[1] Especially when you've been on a plane, blissfully ignorant about the whole thing.

But in spite of some difficulty getting there, the trip was amazing. We spoke at pastors' conferences in Lima. We coordinated some kids' programs with great success. We traveled with bags of rice and beans to the shantytowns outside the city. We carried the bags door to door and introduced ourselves to locals, asking them how they were doing and how we could pray for them. We met people in some of the most horrific conditions I'd ever seen. We were just grateful to help a bit. We were also startled by their infectious joy, even in the midst of such hunger.

Now, I have a hard enough time even speaking English, so my Spanish is pretty terrible.[2] Every conversation happened through translators. On our last night in Peru, some of the Peruvian folks we'd been serving alongside started talking to our host, who was also our translator. I remember watching them going back and forth. Our host kept shaking his head and saying, "No!"

---

[1] Later, Lynn told me she thought it was really me. My poor bride! Me getting into trouble is *always* within the realm of possibility. Please pray for her.

[2] It should be noted that the only thing I learned in high school Spanish class was, "*Senora, mi permite ir al baño?*" Let the reader understand.

Peruvians tend to be passionate. That calm American "no" wasn't stopping anybody. I thought I'd step in and help out the situation (mistake number one). When I asked what was going on, our host started explaining, "They want to honor you guys because you're missionaries and pastors." But before he could say another word, I piped up, "Absolutely! They want to honor us? Let's not make this a thing." Our host shook his head violently and said, "No, you don't understand!" But instead of listening, I insisted. "Oh, come on, it's okay!" (mistake number two).[3]

At this point, I didn't know how they wanted to honor us, but I expected it would be pretty awesome. The Peruvians were also quite excited about it all, which brought even more joy to my heart. They were excited to bless us as we had blessed them. This was going to be fun!

Our Peruvian friends wanted to honor us by serving us a delicacy. It was called *cuy*. And I'm like, "Oh, cuy, great!" But, of course, I had no idea what that was, and I could only think about how amazing this meal was going to be. I expected this delicacy to be savory and otherworldly. I just could not wait for mealtime! As a boy growing up in an all-Italian family in New Jersey, I was taught from a young age that I needed to eat whatever was offered to me. (Following through on that? Mistake number three.)

You might be laughing now because you already know what cuy is. In case you don't (deep breath), cuy is guinea pig. A deep-fried flattened guinea pig—head, paws, every-

---

[3] Actually, in hindsight, this makes for a great story, but when it happened, it wasn't that great. But go ahead and read on; I think you'll like the rest of the story.

thing.[4] All our host could say, fighting back laughter, was, "I tried to tell you, Fusco."

In Peru, cuy is an esteemed food—too much of a delicacy for most people who live there to eat except on special occasions. It's not like a hamburger or something. So when I found out how special it was, I realized I *had* to eat the cuy or it would be horribly offensive to our hosts.

I know you're all wondering how the cuy tasted, and I don't host a show like *Bizarre Foods* or anything, so let me just say, you know how it tasted! [5]

So you could say I learned my lesson. Now I know that if I'm on the missions field and someone wants to honor me with some special food, I'll ask what it is first. And if my translator is saying, "No!" I might even take his advice.

Talk about expectations. This food was a delicacy, so I expected that at the least it would look weird but taste amazing (and I'm sure it did to some people), but it was totally unappetizing to me.

Great Expectations

Sometimes, unmet expectations are funny—like a mouthful of cuy when you were expecting . . . not cuy. But things don't always work out the way we expect. No matter who you are or what your story is, I can guarantee you there's at least one thing we all hate: the disappointment when things go in a way we don't want or expect.

---

[4]   Now, I'm not recommending this, but if you want to search for an image on Google of what I'm describing, I won't stop you.

[5]   If you absolutely love cuy, God bless you. Please don't be mad at me. But, to my credit, I am consistent—I don't like *pet* guinea pigs either.

You know what I mean. I'm sure you have your stories of failed expectations that range from distressing to pleasantly surprising. We all do. We've all had moments when we've thought, *That was not how this was supposed to go*. Sometimes these experiences make up the most devastating moments of our lives: the loss of a loved one, the ending of a relationship, a failed business venture or career move, a child's tragic life choices, or our *own* tragic life choices.

As we explore another movement toward crazy happy together, you will be surprised. Our next beatitude/fruit of the Spirit pairing won't be quite what we expected. Read the verses that started this chapter again. Think about the implications here! Not only is Jesus saying mourning and joy go together, he's saying mourning *produces* joy in the kingdom of God. That's a provocative statement.[6]

It might sound counterintuitive, but what Jesus has to say to us here is one of the most comforting promises in all of Scripture for the brokenness we experience. Now, all of us have different backgrounds and histories, different hurts and issues. But life is still messy for each and every one of us, and Jesus is real in the midst of the mess.

What Jesus has to say about mourning and joy is revolutionary for the way we understand grief: in your life and in this world, there is so much brokenness. Most of us expect joy to come through the *absence* of brokenness. But what Jesus teaches us is that joy comes from lives that allow God to meet us and work *through* brokenness.

As we are beginning the journey through both the Beatitudes and the fruit of the Spirit, there is something I want

---

[6] But let's be real, it's not unusual for Jesus to be provocative.

you to take notice of. Jesus's teaching in the Beatitudes builds on itself. There's a natural progression that happens. This is also true within the fruit of the Spirit.

Aside from the fact that *no one* other than Jesus would ever say, "How fortunate are those who mourn," what you'll notice is this: our poverty leads to mourning. This makes sense. In the same way, love leads to joy. But let's unpack it further.

When we come to Jesus in spiritual poverty, in our own spiritual bankruptcy, we see our personal brokenness and all the injustices of the world we live in. But our awareness of brokenness doesn't necessarily affect all of us in the way Jesus is describing. You can very easily see brokenness and still have a cold, hard heart. In fact, the magnitude of the brokenness we see on a daily basis can have the opposite result and desensitize us to the pain of others *unless* we allow the Spirit of God to move us.

Desensitization is increasing throughout our culture. My parents told me about the days not long after the first images of the Vietnam War popped up on TV sets. The images of bodies and violence coming back home were so provocative that they created an almost instantaneous anti-war movement in America. It's one thing to have a war at a distance; it's another to see it in your living room.

Fast-forward about fifty years, and the amount of violence the average American sees in a day from news and entertainment sources is so intense that we don't even bat an eye at it anymore. Not to mention we have smartphones in our pockets 24/7 with those images. It's as if we're so used to the fact that everything's jacked up that we hardly register it anymore. It doesn't increase our heart rate even a little bit.

That's a problem the Bible calls "hardness of heart."[7] We stop being moved by what should move us.

God hates callous hearts. Why? Because he wants us to be truly human, which means more like him, since we're made in his image. Contrary to many ideas about God that paint him as unfeeling or unmoved by pain and evil, God is moved by the suffering of others. We deny his image and our own humanity by our lack of feeling in the face of such pain. In his kingdom, the poverty and brokenness we see in ourselves and our world is meant to actually drive us right into authentic feelings of mourning and grief.

Take a minute to reflect. When was the last time you truly *mourned* the suffering in the world? When was the last time it caused you to take action beyond just clicking "Share" on Facebook? The harsh reality is that we reveal our hardness of heart when we no longer feel others' suffering.

I'll be honest—I'm aware of my own heart-hardness. Every day, I'm inundated with another set of stories, another set of tragedies, another set of graphic videos with real live blood and gore, and it's desensitizing. I go numb.

It's easy to get overwhelmed when we see patterns in society and ourselves that have no place in the kingdom of God. This is where the *progression* of the Beatitudes (which I mentioned earlier) becomes super important. Remember, entrance into God's kingdom begins with awareness of our spiritual poverty, and if we forget where we've come from, we won't be able to love people going forward.

The kind of spiritual poverty that produces the fruit of love in our lives is also what keeps our hearts soft and able to

---

[7]   Mark 16:14.

mourn the brokenness in ourselves and the world. And that's where change—and joy!—really starts.

There's an old saying among churchy people: "Love the sinner and hate the sin." In a sense, this is right on. People are more than just what they do. But I want to take it a step further in regard to this beatitude and turn that phrase a bit for you: What if the better step is for you to love the sinner and hate *your* sin?

I know. Another "Ouch, Fusco" moment. When we look at life that way, we're no longer saying, "I love everybody, and I hate what they do"; we're saying, "I love everybody, and I hate what I do." God wants us to prioritize our personal responsibilities so our job becomes twofold: to love people and battle our own sin.

When that happens, change is exponential. As God transforms our lives, we become transformation agents in other people's lives because we're doing battle against our own junk. Jesus's way of transforming the world is transforming one person at a time, starting with removing our own beams so that we can help with others' specks.

Take pornography and sex trafficking, two huge systemic problems in today's world. If there were no people willing to pay for sex with an exploited person, there'd be no sex-trafficking industry. And if there were no pornography, the dark and exploitative sexualization of our culture would decrease, and sex trafficking would experience less exponential growth. So, yes, we must try to eradicate sexual slavery, but at the same time, there's a demand problem: we realize that because there is a demand, somebody in a fallen world will fulfill the supply, and they'll use all sorts of evil ways to do that.[8] We must look at ourselves and ask, "What can I do differently so that I help lessen the demand?" Sure, we may never dabble in these things, but we can see lustful or exploitative motives in our hearts and actions. By dealing with our own garbage, we are actually part of the solution.

Sin is usually that way, isn't it? One thing leads to another, things go downhill, and it's all bad. That's why we have to look closely at our own lives. Each of our desires is driving something in this world. We need to guard our hearts.

Thankfully, God's plan doesn't stop with mourning. He's not interested in us walking around sad and grief-stricken all the time. He's not trying to lead us into lives of despair and misery. The blessing Jesus promises for those who mourn is that they will be comforted.

If you're like me, you might be a little confused right now, because if our poverty leads to mourning, and mourning leads to comfort, what exactly is the point?

Here's a truth bomb for you: we love the outcome, but God loves the process. You see, Jesus is revealing part of God's ongoing plan of redemption for the world—that even in our present reality, God is beginning to leverage the brokenness of the world and bring beauty from ashes, joy from sadness. His ongoing redemptive work starts with our soft hearts, broken for what we see, and our mourning drives us into the arms of the Lord, where he comforts the brokenhearted. That comfort we receive becomes the comfort we

---

[8] Do some reading on this if you're interested. A great resource is https://endsexualexploitation.org/responses. The reality of what I'm getting at here is sobering and, to me, mind blowing.

can offer to others. And this is how God can redeem even the most horrific situations through his children. (Our problems are not pointless; our problems are purposeful in the hands of God.)

Talking about suffering always raises questions about God's place within it, so let me be clear: God is never the source of the evil we endure in life. Nor is he handcuffed by it. He allows it.

Because God's ways are infinitely higher than ours, that means his imagination is too. And the Lord can imagine ways to work in our lives in the midst of suffering, even when it seems impossible to us that anything beautiful could come out of the tragedies we endure. This is one of the keys to being crazy happy: remembering that God has a plan, even in our most heartbreaking moments.

Learning Through the Loss

I've always said I wish God could teach me the biggest lessons without the biggest heartaches. But I am continually learning that the Lord gets some of his most profound work done in my heart in the context of suffering. I usually find it's seasons of grief and suffering when I learn the most.

More than twenty years later, the tragic loss of my mother to cancer is still one of the most painful parts of my life. She was diagnosed with lung cancer at forty-seven years young. After some gnarly months of treatment, my mother was declared "in remission," only to suffer a shocking relapse and a rapid decline. My mom breathed her last breath on this side of eternity on July 3, 1997.

It shook me to the core. I wasn't your typical mama's boy either. But my mom was one of those larger-than-life people, full of love, vitality, wisdom, and fun. She was my greatest advocate. She had this amazing way of challenging you and cheering you on at the same time. She was amazing at letting you be you while still helping to guide and shape you. For me, it was almost impossible to imagine living in a world without my mom. And I didn't want to.

After her death, I was unsure how this tragedy would affect my family. If mothers are designed to be the glue that holds a family together, my mother felt like more—like some sort of Department of Defense, military-grade, highly classified, too-strong-for-the-public superglue. I was haunted by the thought of *How can we go forward as a family?*

But I have seen us blossom despite my mother's absence. I have watched everyone in my family step in and up in some of the most beautiful ways. My father has grown, as have my sisters and I.

One of the most beautiful and joyful examples of this was when my dad got remarried. My sisters and I adore my father's wife, Marianne. And we were so happy for them both. But my dear grandparents, Anita and Anthony—my mother's parents!—were also there to celebrate this new union. To see them supporting their son-in-law, their deceased daughter's husband, as he began life with a new companion still inspires me. I am sure grateful for my family, and especially my grandparents, for letting their sorrow turn to joy.

Tragedy can present an incredible opportunity for the best parts of our humanity to emerge. If you think about it, the greatest tragedy in history was the cross of Jesus Christ. And God also leveraged Jesus's finished work on the cross to become the greatest triumph in history.

Although the disciples wept at the death of Jesus, their joy was unspeakable at his resurrection. But for the disciples, their joy hinged on accepting the fact that Jesus was who he said he was when he appeared to them after his resurrection.

Some of us are still living in the tragedies we've experienced and are unwilling to receive the comfort of Jesus. I lived that way for a long time. When my mother passed away, I was in that spot. I didn't understand, and her death felt wrong in every possible way. But what I didn't realize was that God was seeking to do a restorative and resurrecting work in my life. And although at that time I was unwilling because I was still so hurt, it was the beginning of incredible redemption. I believe that God wants to do the same with you.

Jesus is the Great Physician, and a good doctor doesn't impose himself on you. He offers his treatment plan, and as the patient, you can either accept it or reject it and go in a different direction.

See, God doesn't change your tragedy; he changes you *through* the tragedy. He doesn't make it go away; he redeems it. I remember when my mother passed away, someone said, "Daniel, listen, time heals all wounds." But I've learned that, unfortunately, time *doesn't* heal all wounds. Time can make some wounds almost start to feel normal, but only Jesus truly *heals* wounds.

When Jesus heals, he doesn't undo what's been done to us. He takes the wrongs and the pain we've experienced, and he works in his infinite wisdom to *comfort* us. And when we are receptive to his work in the midst of our tragedies, through his perfect care and wisdom, our scars become testimonies of God's faithfulness. And those testimonies are a means for us to comfort others, because we've walked the very path they're on.[9]

There is no life more beautiful than somebody who's lost a loved one and is now helping someone else walk through the grieving process. And there's nothing more beautiful than somebody who's been lost who loves somebody enough to share the good news and walk with the individual through that whole process of learning how to follow Jesus.

Our empathy lacks substance unless we've walked through suffering ourselves with Jesus, unless we have mourned and been comforted by the Lord.

At the beginning of his ministry, Jesus stood and read from Isaiah 61, revealing himself as Israel's anointed savior, the one who would comfort those who mourn and bring them joy[10]:

> The Spirit of the Lord GOD is upon Me,
> Because the LORD has anointed Me
> To preach good tidings to the poor;
> He has sent Me to heal the brokenhearted,
> To proclaim liberty to the captives,
> And the opening of the prison to those who are
>   bound;
> To proclaim the acceptable year of the LORD,
> And the day of vengeance of our God;
> To comfort all who mourn,
> To console those who mourn in Zion,

---

[9] See 2 Corinthians 1:3–4.

[10] See Luke 4:16–21.

To give them beauty for ashes,
The oil of joy for mourning,
The garment of praise for the spirit of heaviness;
That they may be called trees of righteousness,
The planting of the LORD, that He may be glorified.[11]

Through the tragedies of our lives, God can bring comfort. That redemption leads to an outcome we would never expect. He's always in the business of resurrecting and redeeming even the small details of our lives. And what we experience of God's comfort now is just a foretaste, a precursor of Jesus's return, when he will set everything right.

The key for us is to make sure we don't let our hearts get hard in the midst of all the brokenness we see, experience, and endure. It can be incredibly overwhelming! And don't get me wrong, Jesus never condemns us for struggling. He knows we are human. He promises to pour the water of his Spirit over the hard places of our hearts and renew us when we simply invite him to do so.

Now, here's where this gets really fun.

As we suffer and as we mourn, God comforts us, and the fruit of that comfort is what?

Can you guess?

That's right.

Joy.

More Than Happy

Joy is the virtue in the Christian life corresponding to what the rest of the world understands as happiness. But it's not

---

[11] Isaiah 61:1–3.

really happiness at all. On the surface they do seem related. But happiness depends on circumstances, whereas joy does not. Of course, our culture is focused on happiness, and I don't think it's a bad thing. We all want to be happy, don't we? That's natural.

But sometimes it seems Christians think happiness is bad—that we should feel guilty for wanting to be happy. I've never understood that. I mean, if we get only one shot to live this life, we might as well make it a happy one. I like to say there's a reason McDonald's never tried to sell a Sad Meal.

Desiring happiness isn't wrong. But the cultural concept of happiness today is circumstantial, and that can be a problem. In a social-media world like we live in today, each person is weighing his or her life against somebody else's. Even if something wonderful happens in our world today, our happiness is always fleeting because we're on the watch for the next best thing.[12]

This happens all the time, doesn't it? Always the next thing, then the thing after that. It's like when you are in high school. Halfway through, you can't wait to finally graduate. Then you head to college, but halfway through, you can't wait to be done with school and get a J-O-B. Then you finally start working, and sure enough, you start longing for retirement.

The same thing happens when people buy houses (everyone's heard of "buyer's remorse") or when they get that first scratch on their new car. Because let's face it: our ideas of

---

[12] I won't get on a soapbox about social media, as I wholeheartedly believe there are tons of opportunities to use social media in a beautiful way, and I try to do that myself. But when we spend an inordinate amount of time on social media, it feeds into our comparison culture.

happiness are not born in the right places. So how can we expect them to satisfy? The key to a happiness that isn't fleeting is actually joy born out of trust in God.

If you let your spiritual poverty lead to mourning and then let God comfort you in the midst of that mourning, the joy that arises won't be based on your circumstances but rather on a disposition of your heart—a confidence that God has good plans for you, no matter what else goes on. My friends, *that* is joy!

And that's why it says in Nehemiah 8:10, "The joy of the LORD is your strength."

Think about that! Not our self-confidence or our great choices. No, our joy is sourced in who God is—that he is good and powerful and in control. Not to mention, God is the most joyful person you will ever meet.

God wants to bestow true joy on all who believe in Jesus. This is a deep-flowing joy, based in a reality beyond any circumstances we find ourselves in. Let that marinate for a second! We can have an inner state that is incredibly, joyfully out of keeping with even the most difficult situations we face. This isn't denying trouble in our lives; it's triumphing over it.

I want to share with you a great definition of joy I learned from an amazing theology teacher called the Sunday school classroom.[13] Many of our kids know this definition, but so often we forget it as adults.

---

[13] The best way to give yourself the most solid foundation in your faith is to teach Sunday school. Anytime we understand a concept well enough to break it down for kids, we can rest assured we've internalized it ourselves.

Joy can be broken down into three parts: Jesus, Others, and Yourself.[14]

This shows us the order that leads to real joy. And it's as crazy as all these countercultural ways that God loves to work in us. With that definition in place, right away we see the problem with pursuing happiness any way other than how Jesus invites us to. Our culture uses the exact opposite order for joy. Our world says it's you, then others, then Jesus (or religion), right? Our culture says, "You do you," and that you should then make room for others *if* (and that's a big "if") you have anything left.

Except, guess what? When you do you and you come first, you hardly ever have meaningful room in your life for anybody else. Others tend to become a commodity that you use for you. Left to its own devices, our "flesh"—the small, selfish part of us—is never satisfied. It's as though everyone exists to serve you, and you never actually get around to serving others. Of course, from there you definitely *don't* want to go to Jesus, because his answer is always going to be counterintuitive. If you want to find happiness, you need to die to yourself. If you want that deep joy you long for, you need to be like Christ and put God first, then others, *then* yourself.

It's really hard to die to yourself when you're trying to live for yourself, isn't it?

And don't miss the fact that our culture is one of the most statistically unhappy cultures ever. If you don't believe me, just read some of the psychological research coming out these days. We have more access to information, knowledge,

---

[14] In case you are bad at acronyms, this spells *joy*.

food, and comfort than at any other time in the history of mankind, yet our culture is radically unhappy.

It's really hard to die to yourself when you're trying to live for yourself.

Why is that? It's because we're not following God's way to joy. And God's way to joy is to put Jesus first. (And so far the Beatitudes and the fruit of the Spirit are rolling along beautifully. Isn't it amazing how God's Word works?)

Check this out. When we understand the brokenness of the world and our own spiritual bankruptcy and we mourn and Jesus comforts us, we decide to roll with Jesus. And then Jesus teaches us that if we want to love him, we can do so by loving other people. And that means our own self-styled, self-centered interests usually come in last place. But in return we receive God's infinite joy.

As we continue to pursue what it means to live crazy happy, we can start here, with an acknowledgment that the joy of the follower of Jesus is a brokenhearted joy.

Christ himself is the ultimate example of brokenhearted joy. Jesus wept at Lazarus's tomb even though he knew he was going to raise him from the dead. He wept in the Garden of Gethsemane but endured the Cross. Why? "For the joy set before him."[15] Jesus knew that the way to crazy happy joy went through the mourning of the Cross. The gift of new life

---

[15] Hebrews 12:2 (NIV).

that brings joy to the world comes through the suffering and pain of Golgotha (the place where Jesus was crucified).

And even though we know the world is broken, we need to let it break our hearts. And we need to make sure we don't try to shield ourselves from the grief that a broken world produces. Don't let your heart become hard toward the things that break God's heart. Our mourning is a catalyst for God's transformative work in our hearts and for how we live in the world.

When we as the people of God begin to live differently, God's joy is our strength. Because of what Jesus has done, joy begins to flow through our lives into a world that is joy-less. And so it brings us back once again to the reality that God is looking for people just like us who want to let him reign in our lives.

The reign of God never stays private; he is always going public. But right now, it looks different from what we might expect. It's quieter, more subtle. But God wants to go public in our community and in our world through you and me, even with our brokenness and our pain and our struggles. And actually? Through them! Because God's comfort trans-forms the greatest tragedies into the places of Jesus's greatest victory.

Yeah, with people, it's impossible. But with God, *all* things are possible. So as we dig into this beautiful life of crazy hap-piness, start here, today. Allow the God of the all-possible to comfort you and walk with you every day into a place of deep, abiding joy.

This kind of joy will look different from what you've al-ways been told. That's why it can transform your life—and maybe even transform the world.

4

The Crazy Happy Way of Peace

Blessed are the meek,
For they shall inherit the earth.

—Matthew 5:5

The fruit of the Spirit is . . . peace.

—Galatians 5:22

I once heard a story about John D. Rockefeller. After Rockefeller became the world's first billionaire in 1916, a reporter asked him, "How much more money do you want to make?" His response?

"Just a little bit more."

Now, I'll never be a billionaire. I can't fathom making that much money, and I can't say I'd care to. (Sounds stressful.) But Rockefeller's response to this reporter brings up a question we all ask in different ways. Here it is: *Am I enough?*

When you look at the things in your life you don't understand, it always boils down to that core question:

- *Am I smart enough?*
- *Am I secure enough?*
- *Am I good-looking enough?*
- *Am I healthy enough?*
- *Have I done a good enough job to deserve love?*
- *Am I successful enough?*

In all honesty, I think that question of being enough fuels the bulk of the insecurity we experience. No matter what happens in life, we want to know that we're secure in something and have a means of belonging.

If you really think about the question, the very fact that we ask *Am I enough?* invites us into a deeper reality we like to avoid. See, the only reason a person asks that (and, remember, we all do) is because in our heart of hearts, we already know the answer to the question.

We know that we aren't enough. The little voice inside never really shuts up about it:

- *You're not good-looking enough.*
- *You're not healthy enough.*
- *You're not smart enough.*
- *You're not enough.*

I get it. This is super heavy to think about. Real talk. That's why we love to avoid it at all costs. And if the story were to end there, life would be horribly depressing, wouldn't it?

Thankfully, that's not the end of the story. True, we are not enough. And, my friends, that is exactly why we believe in Jesus. In our lack, Jesus comes and says to us through his Spirit, "You were weighed in the balance and found wanting.

You don't have it all together. On your best moment of your best day, you are radically in need, and you are not enough. But guess what? *I am.* You are indwelt by my Spirit, and you are worth it."

That reality changes everything else we experience, because if our sufficiency (or lack thereof) is at the root of all our insecurities, we've got something amazing to say to all our fears. We don't have to worry about being enough if we already know we're not *but that Jesus is.* And if we grab hold of the sufficiency of Jesus, it transforms our insecurities into invitations.

> One of the things I love so much about Jesus is that he's not scared of who we are. He knows. And he wants to make us beautiful in his sight.

Now, don't miss this! Let me say it again: *Jesus wants to transform our insecurities into invitations.* Every time we feel insecure, it's actually like a message from Jesus inviting us closer. How awesome is that?

One of the things I love so much about Jesus is that he's not scared of who we are. He knows. And he wants to make us beautiful in his sight.

Our culture is so absolutely scared of real humanity. We try with everything we are not to appear weak or flawed. We are ashamed, even of what we cannot help. We are scared of who we really are because deep down we feel we're always coming up lacking. Have you ever become exhausted trying to make yourself feel as though you're enough? I know I have. And then we begin to play games with ourselves. We tell ourselves all kinds of different lies to try to fortify our false sense of self-sufficiency, which is impossible to stabilize.

But then Jesus comes along. And when he moves into our lives, we realize that every time we ask, "Am I good enough? Am I smart enough? Do I have enough? Am I enough? Am I deserving of anything?"—we are driven right into his arms. (Or we should be!) In the presence of our Savior, we begin to realize that in our weakness, his strength is made perfect. In our feelings of insecurity, the anchor of his strength holds.

Meekness, Not Weakness

Have you noticed that, by our logic, just about everything Jesus teaches is topsy-turvy? In the world we live in, his equations don't make any sense—at least not at first. And this point is one of those places where we go, *Huh?* Our security comes only through an acknowledgment of our insecurity? The way to life is through death? The way to abundance is through self-denial?[1] The way to peace is through meekness?

Once again, we find Jesus and his message taking us to a place our culture doesn't want to go.

By now you've likely noticed that what God sees as beauti-

---

[1]   This is why I love Jesus so much. No matter how much you think about his words, there is always a deeper level to them.

ful is almost never what we would see as beautiful. What he says will lead to the happiness we long for feels, well, backward. In fact, Jesus's teaching becomes downright subversive so often because his kingdom is vastly different from any location or time in the world. What culture, in all the history of the world, has manifested these "backward" practices as a way of life and victory?

We're about to see Jesus get subversive again, because he now identifies another blessed person—the one who is meek—and I don't know about you, but I never hear that word used culturally, not even occasionally. But Jesus thinks a meek person is beautiful, and he is telling us that the way to cultivate a fulfilling life is through meekness.

Meekness might not be a word you'll hear in contemporary Western vernacular, but probably most of us do have an idea what it means. And we probably think of it as weakness.

I want to start here: meekness is not weakness.

Our culture believes that any sort of humility, any lack of self-promotion, is a sign of weakness—we've already hit on that theme. Anytime we meet people who are self-effacing in any sort of way, we begin to think they're weak because they seem unconfident. But it's not true.

Meekness gets at the absence of any sort of pretentiousness and suggests not only a gentleness but also self-control. In fact, theologian William Barclay said that meekness is strength under control.[2] I love that picture. See, the strongest person in a room is not the person who snaps and shows ev-

---

[2]   William Barclay, *The Gospel of Matthew*, vol. 1 (Philadelphia: Westminster Press, 1958), 91–93.

eryone how strong he is. The strongest person is the one who has all the strength in the world but can handle the situation and chooses not to because he picks his battles.[3]

It's funny, but I'm seeing this played out daily in such a beautiful way in my living room. My son, Obadiah, is just about to start high school,[4] but already he's wearing my clothes and legitimately fitting in them. He's got bigger feet than I do![5] And he's got the beginnings of a little mustache going. I keep telling him, "You're going to have a beard and dreads before you know it." He, of course, hates that idea. So Obadiah (or "O," as I like to call him) is at that age now where he's significantly physically stronger than his two younger sisters. But what I love is that he rarely uses his strength to his advantage with his sisters, because he loves them. That's the definition of meekness.

Let's put meekness into the schematic we've been building within the Beatitudes already. If you're poor in spirit, it will lead you to mourn. Then meekness is simply settling into the reality that you have allowed God to divorce you of your self-focus. Really, what it boils down to is looking at yourself and being willing to truly acknowledge that you're not enough.

---

[3] You want another definition of meekness? Take the word *meek,* and put a hyphen in the middle: *ME-EK*. Like "Me? Ick!" It's pretty good, right?

[4] It's hard to believe I'm the parent of a teenager. I don't know how that happened.

[5] I actually started to buy funky-looking socks, what I call "Dad socks," because I got tired of not having any clean socks since he kept taking mine!

Even though our culture doesn't value meekness, don't miss the fact that Jesus characterized himself as meek. Let's take a look at Matthew 11:28–30: "Come to Me, all you who labor and are heavy laden, and I will give you rest. Take My yoke upon you and learn from Me, for I am gentle and lowly in heart, and you will find rest for your souls. For My yoke is easy and My burden is light."

Jesus, in his perfection, in his incarnation, still knew that the Father was everything. Jesus was willing to be born in a manger instead of a castle. Even though he could have ridden into Jerusalem on a white stallion as a victorious king in his triumphal entry, he chose to ride on a lowly donkey. And he would rather be surrounded by tax collectors and sinners than the greatest minds of his day, because he knew what really mattered. It was the pleasure of his Father, of his life being beautiful in the eyes of God.

As a result, everyday people loved to hang out with Jesus. Little kids thought he was the coolest guy around. Tax collectors loved to be around him, even though he didn't join in when they expressed their rebellion against God. The way Jesus carried himself—in meekness and lowliness—was inviting to people from all different walks of life. The way he lived was an invitation to everyone he encountered to participate in the beauty of the life of God himself.

And, brothers and sisters, if you are in Christ and are truly embracing with your heart and lifestyle all that God is for us in Christ, meekness becomes a default characteristic of who you are.

One of the greatest blessings in my life is my bride, Lynn. And if there was an adjective I would use to describe her, it would be *meek*. My wife is someone I would consider to be a textbook example of meekness:[6] strength under control.

After we married, I moved this sweet, angelic California girl to the East Coast. She joined me in New Jersey, where I was already a few years into starting a church in New Brunswick, home to my alma mater, Rutgers University.[7] It was a rude awakening for this poor girl, you know? First she got married to me, and that's a rude awakening in and of itself. Then add to that the environment of New Jersey, a somewhat feral place where we used to joke that the weak are killed and eaten.[8]

I remember when she tried starting a women's ministry out east. She got major pushback from some of the women in the church. They couldn't decide if they trusted her yet. But she stayed so mellow, so calm. Some of these women tried to treat my wife in the way only people from New Jersey can truly appreciate, and Lynn handled it like a champ. But I remember one of them finally said, "You know what I realized about your wife? Meekness is not weakness. Your wife's a strong woman." And I said, "Yeah, she is, but she just doesn't need to show it."

In our insecurity, we want to flex our strength to mask our weakness. In our insecurity, we want to take the best pictures with our tummies sucked in and little bicep veins popping.

---

[6]   Earlier, I told you that my son, Obadiah, displays meekness as well. He gets that from his mom.

[7]   Go RU Scarlet Knights—Fusco, Class of 1998.

[8]   Of course, there wasn't really cannibalism there. Just a lot of strong personalities and Dunkin' Donuts.

Everything we do is to show how strong we are. But for the child of God, all of that is a sham. And we know it's a sham.

When we live meekly, we are willing to be quiet when our instincts tell us to throw an insult back at that person who is coming at us. We are willing to hold our tongues even when we have the *perfect* retort on Twitter to that public figure we hate (and we know we're missing out on some serious likes). Meekness causes us not to join in to the usual gossip at school or work or to withhold one-upping someone for love's sake.

To live meekly, our lives are properly governed by the Spirit of God. Never lashing out. Never in a scared panic. Never harmfully aggressive. Always strong. Full of faith. Exceedingly welcoming. Ultimately, meekness means holding space, as Jesus would have, in every situation we find ourselves in.

So let's not miss the tail end of what Jesus says here: "Blessed are the meek, for they shall *inherit the earth*." This part is so cool. What this means is that biblical strength will be victorious.[9]

Naturally, our culture says that the strong, the aggressive, the harsh, the tyrannical—they are the ones who will inherit the earth. The government with the most bombs, the biggest

---

[9] It's confession time for me. There was one place I heard of meekness before I heard it in the Bible, and that was from the very controversial American theologian Frank Zappa. I'm not recommending listening to Frank Zappa, okay? Unless you get his instrumental stuff, you don't have to worry about it. Some of the lyrics are, shall we say, inappropriate. But he had a song called "The Meek Shall Inherit Nothing." (So if by chance you were looking for an easy example of Jesus and Frank Zappa's many differences of opinion, that's one right there.)

army, the greatest tanks, the top technology—they're going to be the victorious ones.

Per usual, Jesus is teaching us the opposite of what we would think automatically, and he's actually quoting the Old Testament here. Check out Psalm 37:11:

> The meek shall inherit the earth,
> And shall delight themselves in the abundance of—

Of what?

Peace.

Why? Because the *fruit* of meekness is peace. Peace is the natural outflow, the product of a meek life.

The Architect of Peace

It's no coincidence the fruit of meekness is peace. What's actually going on here is we're seeing evidence of the fact that the Spirit of God is the most amazing architect. We're in a place where God's Word begins to crystallize into the most powerful, intricate whole.

Psalm 37:11 puts meekness and peace together. The same thing happens when you place the third beatitude next to the third characteristic of the fruit of the Spirit. (God's Word is breathtaking, isn't it?)

Strength under control—meekness—is victorious. Why? Because when we focus our attention on what is material, we focus on our own strength to acquire what is temporary (money, power, attention, reputation, clout) to help mask our insecurity. When we do that, we're grasping at what is momentary, not what is eternal. And what is momentary will never be victorious. It can't be. Our souls are too big to be satisfied by such small things, because they can't bring peace.

But if I'm honest, I spend so much time grasping at what is temporary. I often believe the values of our culture over the values of the kingdom. And when I do, I miss out. And you do, too, when you live this way, because the meek receive a *greater* inheritance. The "earth" in Psalm 37:11 is referencing the inheritance of the children of Israel. It's "the land," which isn't just a place or the planet. "The earth" is a symbol of a whole way of life in holy abundance. It's God's people finally stepping into the role they were made to fill. It's foreshadowing a great inheritance bigger than the whole world as we know it: the new heavens and the new earth that God has promised to the followers of Jesus.

Meekness draws us into this reality of what it means to be in Christ. I see the progression of these teachings continuing here. See, if you're poor in spirit, your own poverty leads you to mourn, and then your mourning leads you to treat others without any sort of aggression or harshness, and your strength is under control. Now, all of a sudden, the peacemaking God who has made peace with us empowers us to be people of peace in the world.

Let's get nerdy for a second, shall we? (I think you'll like this.) The word *peace* in Greek was the way people greeted one another. It carried the same idea as the Hebrew word *shalom*. *Shalom* is a word that depicts reality—the way everything *ought* to be. It's everything working, *really* working. It's well-being in its most ultimate sense—nothing missing, nothing broken.

One of my favorite British theologians, John Lennon

(*wink*), had it right when he told us to give peace a chance.[10] But he also had it so wrong. I mean, let's be real: he couldn't even keep peace between the Beatles! But we can't really blame good ol' John, because real peace comes only from a right relationship with God. Shalom is a natural hunger for humans, but it can be satisfied only in God.

When we live for self, it tears peace apart, because that choice, as "good" as we tell ourselves it feels, is not how the world is supposed to work! When we put our trust in Jesus and we have God's peace, God totally changes the way we make decisions, because we finally see how it all fits together. We realize that it's actually not about me. It's actually not about you. It's about *God* and his good earth, which has gotten mangled by all these mistakes we keep making. It's about finding a place of peace where we can live in harmony.

I realize that each of us is in process and that we are all on different steps on our respective journeys. And some of you remain unconvinced. You think it is silly to think that not everyone is at peace with God. Maybe you're one of those people who has bought into the notion of our culture that by nature of being alive, you are entitled to God being good with you. But that's another failing of an entitlement culture. Where in God's Word does it say, "Because you're alive, we good"?

Let me make it more personal, because I really want to press on this. Let's say you're married. Or if you're not mar-

---

[10] At this point, you may have noticed that I like to joke that musicians are theologians. And they truly are. Musicians tell people, through song, what they ought to think about God and life. I'm not saying they are good or necessarily biblical theologians. But they are, in fact, practicing theology.

ried, let's say you're in a committed relationship, okay? And your significant other says, "Hey, listen, I'm just going to go out and mess around with all these other people. We cool, right?" I'm guessing you're *not* actually cool with that, unless you really don't care about that person and he or she is just part of your side hustle that you got going on. But that's not love anyway.

So if that's the case, if you're really *not* good with someone doing whatever he or she wants to do in your relationship, why would you think God's cool with us doing whatever we want? It's not even logical. It's not even realistic, on any level. Now, I feel I can speak directly about that because I lived that way for much of my life.

So here's the good news for all of us: because of the peace with God that Jesus bought for us on the cross, we also receive the gift of inner peace. Check out Philippians 4:7: "The peace of God, which surpasses all understanding, will guard your hearts and minds through Christ Jesus."

See? The *upward* peace we have with God now leads to an *inward* peace because his universal shalom now guards not only our hearts but our minds, in Jesus.

Once you have upward peace and inward peace, it leads to outward peace, where you and I become people of peace in a world that is broken. And that peace changes lives. It changes families. It changes communities.

God himself longs to see everything in his creation working together, all humanity linking up hands with him to get his will done on earth. When we live in the world as people of meekness and peace, God's beautiful and good but broken world starts to get transformed.

That's why Jesus said, "Peace I leave with you, My peace I

give to you; not as the world gives do I give to you. Let not your heart be troubled, neither let it be afraid."[11]

Isn't it true that when our hearts are troubled and we're fearful, we become not agents of peace but agents of discord? That's what happens when we miss the meekness of Jesus in our lives.

In all this, I think it's important to remember that the Beatitudes are not about doing better or trying harder.

Remember how we started this chapter?

Jesus is enough.

Jesus has done it already.

The beautiful life of being crazy happy is about you and me learning how to abide in Jesus. Yes, even in the real world that we face every day. Yes, so honestly that we can acknowledge that even though we don't have it all together, Jesus is enough.

Because Jesus has completed the work I could never do, I can truly rest. Even though life is hard, I can walk in Jesus's strength in my life by his Spirit. And I can get over myself so that God's plans can come to pass in my life and in the lives of those I encounter.

I love the example of Abraham, the great father of faith. Remember when he and Lot were fighting over land and they needed to separate? God had promised Abraham the land, but Abraham said, "Lot, you choose. You can choose what you want. All this land is before us. Which one do you want?"[12]

See, in our culture, we say, "I'm going to choose first.

---

[11] John 14:27.

[12] See Genesis 13.

We're going to draw straws. We're going to play roshambo,[13] best two out of three." We have to make sure we get what we want. But Abraham didn't worry about the choices of others, because he knew the God he served. He knew his God was good and would do good by him no matter what decision Lot made. If you know the story, you know that Abraham took the land Lot didn't want, but Lot ended up in Sodom and Gomorrah. All sorts of messy stuff went on there, and Abraham had to go rescue him.[14]

But isn't that the heart of a peacemaker? A peacemaker says, "I serve a good God. I serve a God who's made peace for me. I have a peace that surpasses all understanding. It's going to work out all right no matter what, so I can take a step of faith."

You see how that works? When we trust the character of God, we not only get to experience God's peace in our own lives, but we also become people of peace equipped to step out in the world, bringing the refreshment of Christ's life with us.

---

[13] Roshambo? Maybe you know it by its more descriptive name, Rock, Paper, Scissors.

[14] Don't miss the fact that even Abraham didn't do this perfectly. A few chapters and many years later, you find him taking matters into his own hands when the Lord didn't give him a son in the time he thought he should. I bring this up because I think it takes pressure off for all of us. Yes, we want to make choices that demonstrate our trust in the character of God—that's how we ought to live. But we don't get it right 100 percent of the time—not because we don't love God but because we aren't perfect. And that's okay. God meets us not with condemnation but with compassion in those moments.

5

The Crazy Happy Way of Patience

Blessed are those who hunger and thirst for righteousness,
For they shall be filled.
—Matthew 5:6

The fruit of the Spirit is . . . longsuffering.
—Galatians 5:22

When I was in college, I purchased my first upright bass. I'd been playing electric bass in bands for years, but one day at a concert, I saw a guy playing an upright bass. His fingers were gliding up and down the strings, and every eye in the room was glued to him. I remember thinking, *Man, that dude is the coolest guy here because of that big old bass.*

At the time, that was my MO—I wanted to do whatever it took to be the coolest guy in the room. I wanted to be the guy at the center of the party, making everyone happy. So, naturally, I did what any reasonable person would do: I went and got myself an enormous upright bass. After my purchase, I realized that those huge upright bass strings are not for the weak of heart!

The first time I ever jammed with my buddies at a gig, I had three massive blisters before we were done with the first set. Smart people would probably take a break at that point until their hands healed, right? Of course they would. Well, I'll leave you to draw your own conclusions, but I just popped those blisters, all three of them, and stuck my hand in hot saltwater. After all, we had two more sets in the gig. Every set I came out with more blisters, so I'd pop them, soak them, and keep playing.

When I got home that night, my hands were more bloody and cracked than I'd ever seen them. (Thanks, upright bass!) So I did what any self-respecting wannabe professional bass player would do: I grabbed some superglue and glued my fingers back together. After all, I had a lesson the next day!

I was studying with the principal bassist in the New Jersey Symphony at the time, and when he saw my superglued fingers, he argued with me and tried to get me to take a day off. But I didn't want to take time off, so we had our lesson as usual. It wasn't easy. I played bass with tears streaming down my face from the pain.

I know you're probably thinking, *Fusco, you're nuts!* In a way, I kind of was. But in another way, it made a lot of sense. I was really trying to get somewhere in my career, so in my mind I had to do what I had to do. I was focused on the end goal. Eyes on the prize. Desire—a powerful motivator.

Desire Drives Us
Think about the things you've desired along life's way, maybe the things you're desiring right now. Those desires drive you,

the decisions you make, and why you make those decisions. One popular world religion, Buddhism, teaches that desire causes us suffering and should be avoided through detachment. But Jesus teaches the opposite.

Listen, the thirsts and the hungers we have are important. As disordered as our lives can become, in the kingdom of God, our deepest desires are God given. And they are aimed at making our lives beautiful and, ultimately, crazy happy. Does this mean that every expression of those desires is healthy? No. But wanting good things is, well, *good*.

> Our deepest desires are God given. And they are aimed at making our lives beautiful and, ultimately, crazy happy.

As we take this journey to discover what constitutes a beautiful life, we find that Jesus doesn't want us to *get rid of* our desires; he wants us to *seek him* for their fulfillment. Why? Because he has a purpose for our longing, a deeper purpose that is the *why* behind our *what*.

To sum this up, our deep desires aren't bad—God created us with them. But we need to make sure they are properly oriented. So, hunger is great! But what we notice right away from Matthew 5:6 is that you and I need to stay hungry for the right things.[1] Why? Because whatever we desire begins to

---

[1] It was so hard for me not to say, "Stay thirsty, my friends!" I must have swapped out that phrase sixteen times. I just need to confess that. If you

drive our lives. My desire to be a musician drove me, through tears, to ignore my own physical pain to perform to the best of my ability. But on the other hand, part of my music-industry life at the time *also* included a desire to party the hardest I knew how to. And that led to some really destructive consequences.

This is why Jesus calls that person blessed who desires righteousness above everything else. All other things fall into place behind that hunger. And just like the consequences I experienced, desiring the ethics of God's kingdom has consequences. But they are *blessed* consequences when in the presence of true righteousness.

So what does this mean? *Righteousness* in this beatitude refers to all things that are right. (I know—obvious. But bear with me.) This includes not only a *personal* righteousness but also righteousness as it pervades society. Societal righteousness is what we call justice—all things in society working rightly together. In other words, Jesus is not simply telling us to be morally upstanding (although, of course, he wants that). But weren't the Pharisees the masters of the moral? Yeah! It was their hypocrisy, by ignoring the demands of true and righteous justice, that put them in danger of Christ's judgment.

Nothing has changed. I'm pretty sure we all agree that we want society to work together in the best way possible. But many of us fail to see that in order to have societal justice, we need to encourage each individual to live rightly before God.

---

know the reference, you know the reference. If you don't know the reference, you definitely don't have to go searching for it, you know what I mean?

Contemporary culture is rightfully passionate about so-cial justice, but too often it doesn't want to look at each in-dividual's choices and responsibilities before a God who is perfectly righteous. And that's the problem.

See, we can't have justice in a culture without personal righteousness too. And the Bible teaches that we can't have individual personal righteousness unless we receive it as a gift from Jesus. So even with our culture's much-desired pas-sion for justice, I think we're trying to get at it the wrong way, and it will never work out in the end.[2]

The gospel informs us that all of us are unrighteous. Maybe we're not as bad as we could be, but we're never as *good* as we should be either. All of us fell. Jesus didn't.

It's a mystery, but when we place our trust in Jesus, his resurrection becomes *our* resurrection. We receive his righ-teousness because he took all unrighteousness upon himself on the cross. Paul said in 2 Corinthians 5:21, "[God] made [Jesus] who knew no sin to be sin for us, that we might be-come the righteousness of God in Him."

It's the great switcheroo, so to speak. (Can I please recom-mend that as a theological term moving forward?)

Jesus, the righteous one. We, who have failed. Our unrigh-teousness traded for his righteousness. The great exchange that transforms our hunger into his.

---

[2] As a side note, I think public shaming is not going to bring justice into this world either. The "thought police," who don't allow people to say what they think or feel, are not going to produce justice throughout a culture. Culture can become just only when righteousness pervades that culture. And that happens only when the individuals who make up the culture receive righteousness as a gift from Jesus. At the end of the day, it's still all about the good news of the gospel of Jesus, just brought into a modern Western social context.

The Power of "No"

The Bible is rich with imagery about our appetites. In Psalm 42:1–2, the sons of Korah wrote,

> As the deer pants for the water brooks,
> So pants my soul for You, O God.
> My soul thirsts for God, for the living God.
> When shall I come and appear before God?

They're describing a deep thirst for God that goes beyond any other desire.

Think about this for a minute. What do you hunger for? What is it that you really want in life? What gets you out of bed in the morning? What keeps you going through the day?[3] Are you staying hungry? Cultivating that holy desire for the things of God?

I am learning that if I'm not intentional about cultivating a hunger for God, I begin to cultivate hunger for other things. We need to keep feeding a holy hunger for the things of God, because if we don't, we will develop other appetites. And I think all of us know what that's like, don't we?

That's also why God says so clearly in his Word that we should not awaken certain appetites before their time. There is a rhythm to desire that needs to come on beat. Basically, whatever you say yes to means you are saying no to something else. Which is great, if it's God's things we're saying yes to. But when we say yes to the wrong appetites, we're often also saying no to the Lord. Instead of feeding a holy hunger,

---

[3]   Other than caffeine, of course.

we're feeding our flesh—the part of us that can so easily distract and hold us back from what is best for us.

But on the other hand, whatever you say no to opens up the opportunity to say yes to something else. So when we deny ourselves, we put ourselves in a position to be in right communion with God, ready to respond to him.

I remember when I first started to follow Jesus. At that time, I had been partying like a rock star for half a dozen years. Most of my days were designed to facilitate the party life. My money was budgeted to provide the necessary party favors. When I look back on it now, it is sad the number of things that I said no to so that I could say yes to getting high.

But as Jesus began to work on me, I found myself starting to find some victory in saying no to drugs and alcohol. It was amazing how many beautiful things I was able to say yes to. Just the time and money alone were worth the change, not to mention the lack of paranoia, social insecurity, and ability to think straight!

Desire always drives us *somewhere*. Sometimes you might think there are things we feel and do that aren't really good or bad. But nothing is neutral. And our desires have the power either to draw us deeper into the Lord's presence or else to pull us away from him. We need to feed the holy hunger.

I always warn people that we have to be very careful with our choices and the habits we build. Our culture is extremely permissive! But just because our culture allows certain things to be legal or permissible, it doesn't mean that those things will bring out the most beautiful parts of our lives. They won't necessarily build God's best into our hearts and lives.

Let's take pornography as an example. Pornography is a

multibillion-dollar industry. But if you take part in it, if you choose to awaken wayward passion and lust through it, porn will drive you away from being able to experience who Jesus is. For real. And it will tarnish your closest, most intimate relationships—the ones that should be the most beautiful. Is it legal in our society? Sure. Is it spiritually powerful? Absolutely—but in the most horrifying ways. And is it good for you? Emphatically, no.

I live in Washington State. Marijuana is legal and increasingly common here. Sometimes as followers of Jesus, we forget that whether or not something is legal isn't really the main issue. Sure, state law is important, but we live by a deeper law. Legality has never been the determining factor in the life of God's people. Cultural permissibility has never been the benchmark for God's vision for a beautiful life. You were never meant to be common. You were never meant to be just like everybody else. You were set apart by Jesus's finished work on the cross and shown a new and better way to live. So, sure, marijuana is legal, but does it draw you closer to Jesus? I have my doubts. Once you're under the influence of anything other than the Holy Spirit, your desires will only draw you away from Jesus.[4]

Another example, if you're outside the bounds of God's covenant of marriage, is sexual intimacy. When you awaken

---

[4] As a pastor in the state of Washington, this is one of those things I get asked about all the time. And I always tell people that sometimes things are lawful but not expedient, as the apostle Paul said. We know how marijuana impairs our judgment and makes it virtually impossible to be right with God, so we can't really imagine how he would desire us to use it, even though it's lawful in some states. Now, if your doctor advises you to use it, I'm not going to give you medical advice. But most of the time, at least in my state, it's not a question of someone's medical needs.

the desire for sexual intimacy outside marriage, it's not as if God thinks the desire is wrong. He created it! It's just not functioning within the authority of Jesus. And outside marriage, awakening that desire actually deadens your senses to the intimate relationship God wants to have with you.

But when we wait for the Lord to fulfill our desires righteously, it can be the most beautiful experience imaginable. Talk about fulfillment. When you make a covenant with your spouse in getting married, all of a sudden you get to experience the fulfillment of all your desires under the authority of Jesus, and within that context, it serves Jesus as an act of worship. I'm not promising a perfect sex life, and neither is God. I'm just saying that the big picture of our God-given desires is good and deeply satisfying.

What we desire, we seek to fulfill. So when we long for the wrong things, we find ourselves little by little (or sometimes with great giant leaps) stepping away from the one thing that will truly give us what we want: the real answer to all our longings.

In Jesus, your desires *will be* fulfilled.

I promise.[5] But if, and *only* if, you desire what can satisfy all lesser desires: a Christlike righteousness that transforms the heart.

Jesus says those who hunger and thirst for righteousness will be *filled*. That's another word for "abundantly satisfied." And not just kinda sorta satisfied; I'm talking about an over-the-top, full-to-the-brim, bursting-forth kind of satisfied. When we stay hungry for the right things, God promises to satisfy the deepest longings of our hearts.

---

[5]   Well, actually, Jesus promised, and I am trusting in his faithfulness.

You may have noticed in your life (I know I've seen it in mine) that when your desires are fleshly, satisfaction is elusive. Even when you get what you want, it's never. quite enough.

Or as another great British theologian (Mick Jagger) said, "I can't get no satisfaction."[6] And he was right! Of course he was, because he was looking for satisfaction in the wrong places.

No amount of money, sex, food, alcohol, drugs, or relationships is ever quite enough. We are always having to up the ante and take it to the next level. This means we're really just spiraling deeper into a pit of unrighteous attempts at numbing instead of addressing our root hunger, which will be found in Christ alone.

But when you hunger and thirst for the righteousness that comes from Jesus, then he says you *will be* filled. I hope you caught that. He's not saying, "I'm telling you there's a chance you may be filled." He's not saying, "You *might* be if you're lucky." No, God promises to truly satisfy the deepest longings of your soul *in* Christ.

Here's the thing. When I say something like that, some of you who have been following Jesus a long time may be thinking, *Actually, I don't agree with you, Fusco. Jesus hasn't given me all the satisfaction I desire.* Hey, I get it. I've been there.

If you're in that place today, you're experiencing an important moment of self-reflection. God wants to do a deeper

---

[6] I can see the dance moves and facial expressions in my mind's eye right now.

work in you. He's not done! And that's good news. He has more planned for you in this process we call "sanctification," the setting apart of your life for Jesus.

Don't feel bad if you don't feel satisfied quite yet. Actually, you should be surprised if you do! It's all part of the journey, the testimony God is writing in your life. Just promise me this: before you lean into the wrong things, lean into the *right* things. Stay hungry for what is good. Feed that hunger. Trust God to keep his promise to fill you. He will.

Just be patient.[7]

The Patience Connection

Because God has given us everything we need in Christ, we begin to see everything else for what it really is: temporary. I know; some things in life are a comfort, but they're not crucial. In Christ, we hold all the temporary things of life with open hands—not as essential but as the window dressing to a deeper, more profound, and more abundant life.[8]

So here's where things get really tricky. God has promised us fulfillment in Christ. And the key to that fulfillment? Patience. So if we want to grow, guess what we have to ask for?

---

[7] We'll talk about that more in a minute.

[8] Sometimes the best way not to get sucked in by our own desires is to look out for someone else's needs instead. If we're staying hungry for the right things, we will start living self-sacrificially and serving others in love. The cool thing that happens from there is that serving gets us out of our own heads and into the reality of what it means to live in the kingdom of God in real time. And as we serve, God grows us in new ways and reveals to us the sweet spot of who he's made us to be. As a result, we become more satisfied the more we serve others.

"No!" (I can hear you screaming it at me.) "Fusco, the absolute *last* thing I want to ask God to give me is more patience!"

I sympathize. That is one of those requests that feels dangerous, right? It feels as if praying that will make every traffic light we approach miraculously turn red. (Or something worse!) But growing in patience isn't just about waiting. Here's the big reveal: patience is the fruit of the Spirit borne of desiring righteousness.

Stay with me. The core definition of *patience*—and I like to use the old-school word for patience, *longsuffering* (for obvious reasons)—is the ability to put up with not having what we want. It's the ability to say, *I'm going to let my life run on somebody else's timetable.* How difficult this is for us depends on what we most deeply want.

Why do we get impatient? Because things are out of our control. Because maybe someone else is running on a different timetable than ours. *Let's go already!* I'm sure you know the feeling I'm talking about. Can we admit that impatience saps some of the crazy happiness out of life?

I experience this "different timetable" situation all the time because I'm always late (and I admit it). Lynn calls it "Italian time."[9] I figure that if I'm within about twenty minutes of when an event starts, I'm on time. However, my wife is German, so if an event starts at noon, you're there at 11:59 or you're late.

My wife is patient when I'm late. But how often do we feel as though God is late or, at the very least, wonder what on

---

[9]   And I'll take whatever excuses she gives me.

earth is the holdup? Are we patient with his sense of timing, which seems to be different from ours?

Our impatience is nothing new. Think about the story of Abraham and Sarah.[10] Remember, God had promised to bless Abraham and make him a father of many nations. Abraham wanted to believe God, but he was old to begin with and kept getting older while he waited on the Lord. His wife, Sarah, was no spring chicken either, and this was long before the advent of modern medicine.[11] So instead of practicing patience with God's timing, they took matters into their own hands, and Abraham had a child, Ishmael, with his wife's servant Hagar. On the surface, it made perfect sense. But that decision caused *all* kinds of problems for him and his descendants.

Of course, God's plan wasn't for Abraham and Sarah to figure out how to fulfill God's plan on their own timetable; God's plan was for them to trust him. More than a dozen years after Ishmael was born, Sarah got pregnant and gave birth to the son God had promised, Isaac. That's right. *Thirteen or fourteen years later.*

Much of the drama within the biblical narratives stems from Abraham and Sarah's lack of patience. Instead of suffering long, they tried to force God onto their calendar. How

---

[10] See Genesis 15–16. Technically, at this point in their lives, they were known at Abram and Sarai. Later on, God changed their names. But since they are most commonly known as Abraham and Sarah, we will use these names.

[11] I love to joke with my older, more seasoned friends about Sarah and Abraham becoming parents at ninety and a hundred years young, respectively. For awkward fun, try that joke yourself.

many times have *you* created an "Ishmael" by not trusting in God's timing? I know I've done it, and I've watched it happen with people I know. I've seen many single people who want so badly to get married, and they start off trusting God to bring them a spouse. But time passes, and God doesn't come through in the manner they thought he would. They get impatient and marry someone even though friends and family warn them they haven't made a good match, or before they fully know who they are. Then they end up with an unhappy marriage and a partner who is not anything like what they were really looking for in a spouse. And they are forced to make the best of a hard situation. It's heartbreaking!

That's why the true fruit of hungering for righteousness is patience. Patience is not the ability to smile and pretend you aren't restless or doubting God's timing; it's the art of owning your impatience and saying, *God, I don't want to wait anymore, but I'm going to slow myself down and get on your timetable.*

If you're about to create an Ishmael, stop. Don't do anything. The key to God doing all that he wants to do in your life is for you to be patient and wait on the Lord.

I know that's incredibly challenging to do. I mean, that's why the New King James and King James versions of the Bible use the word *longsuffering* when referring to patience. It means exactly what it sounds like. Patience is not easy street; rather, it involves suffering for a long time.

In a culture that prioritizes comfort (which isn't inherently a bad thing), we have lost the art of longsuffering. When was the last time an ad on TV told you to pay for something great and then wait to receive it (and who knows how long!)? I don't think so! That ad would go down in flames. Our culture tells us to go after what we want now, exactly how we want it. But we need to reclaim the ability to abide (receive, believe, and trust) and wait for God to do what he wants to do in our lives, believing it to be the absolute preferred outcome for our futures.

The Root of Trust

Let's put this in context with the rest of the Beatitudes. We start with poverty of spirit, which leads to mourning, and then our mourning produces meekness, a strength under control, which leads us to hunger for God to do a fresh work through our lives, which God promises to fulfill. In the same way, the fruit of the Spirit is love, and God's love leads us to joy despite our circumstances. Joy produces peace, and then peace brings us into patience.

What our quality of life really boils down to is that it's rooted in the question "Do you trust God?" Because if we trust him, we can suffer long for him to bring the fulfillment of the right things in our lives. But if we don't trust God, it's impossible to be patient, isn't it?

Without trust that God is who he says he is, there is absolutely no reason to believe that the things you want will ever come to you. When you trust God because you've experienced his love, you can wait on him for anything.

I love the word *trust* because it's different from just belief alone. Belief is an assent of the intellect to say, *I believe this thing to be true.* If I set a kitchen stool down next to you, you would believe you could sit on that stool and the stool would hold your weight. But although you might think, *Fusco, you're a solid guy; I trust the stool will hold me,* and believe that with all your mind, you won't trust until you actually sit down on that stool and pick your feet up.

That's what trust is: belief with feet on it. Trust is belief in action. My friends, the beauty of a heart that suffers long for God's timing is a sweet trust that thrives despite what's going on.[12]

When we trust the Lord, our lives become crazy happy, because trust says, *No matter what I see, I'm going to trust what God has said. No matter how hard the circumstances are, I can trust that he is going to bring beauty out of them. God is going to restore the years the locusts have eaten. He can redeem my life and my mistakes. And he will bring the most amazing things out of it.*

As we seek the crazy happy life, let's root out the misplaced appetites and stay hungry (and thirsty) for the right things. When we demonstrate longsuffering, we learn how to trust God, just like children trust their parents. Life begins to be truly fulfilling when we know we are waiting for God's best as we trust in his timing.

And let's remind ourselves of this: when we came to Jesus, we realized God could be trusted with our past. He can also be trusted with our present. Not only that, but he can be trusted with our future. How awesome is that?

Some of the things you're asking for right now, God may never give you. I believe the same for myself. God's answer to our prayers may be no because he's a good Father and he knows what he's doing. If that's the case, that means he has something better for you than what you would choose for

---

12   Makes me think of Proverbs 3:5–6.

yourself. God's plan for you is so beautifully unique that as you trust him, he will lead you into places you've never dreamed you'd be. And you will learn how to be patient, knowing that in due time, you will reap a harvest.

You will bear the fruit that God has promised to bear in your life if you don't lose heart in the process.

6

The Crazy Happy Way of Kindness

Blessed are the merciful,
For they shall obtain mercy.

—Matthew 5:7

The fruit of the Spirit is . . . kindness.

—Galatians 5:22

One of my earliest memories is of my grandpa putting a football helmet on my head.

Now, if you know me at all, you're aware of how much I love my grandparents. My grandpa was fairly well known in Valley Stream, New York. He was a Pop Warner youth-football coach, and everybody called him Cappy (because you know that when your name is Cappadona, you've got a few too many syllables for the neighbor kids to pronounce).

My grandparents also owned a sweetshop in town. Of course they did—because my grandma is still the sweetest person ever! So they'd go to games, and then everyone would go get egg creams.[1] As a result, I developed this fascination with football and always wanted to play, but my mom wouldn't let me because she felt the game was too violent. (She was ahead of her time.)

Since I couldn't play football, I tried to incorporate what I loved about football into the sports my parents *would* let me play, like soccer and basketball, which is definitely a recipe for a wild ride. In soccer I was a defender, so as you can imagine, I got *really* good at slide tackling people.[2]

Basketball was another story, however, because you're not really allowed to touch anybody. There's no "legal" way to work a little minor violence into the flow of the game. When I first started playing basketball, my dad got roped into coaching because nobody wanted to do it. When he first put me in the game, I fouled out in about two minutes.

"Daniel," my dad said, "you're not really allowed to tackle people in basketball." "Well," I replied, "they got the ball. What else am I supposed to do?" And he's like, "I don't know, but you're not supposed to tackle them."

All this to say, I developed a bit of a reputation in basketball for being just a teensy bit overly outgoing. (Okay, maybe *compulsively overaggressive* would be more accurate.) Needless to say, I didn't have a great basketball career. When the game was getting out of hand, I was the guy they'd throw in to foul the star player five times in thirty seconds, and I'd sit down again. That was basically my job.

---

[1] If you don't know what that is, it is a sweet drink. You have to try one. They are the best.

[2] And, ultimately, getting many yellow and red cards.

Fast-forward. Now I'm a dad with a son who plays basketball. But thankfully for Obadiah, he is way more like my wife than like me. Obadiah is such a kindhearted person that when the other team has the ball, he gives them space to do their thing. I'll never forget, after one of the games, I said, "If you foul out of the game, I'll take you out for dinner."

"Wait. Dad, what?" he replied. "But won't I hurt somebody?"

I told him not to intentionally hurt anybody but just to prevent the other team from getting the ball, no matter what it took. (Telling you this is how I'm confessing my sins and asking you to pray for my kids, okay? Bear with me.)

In most situations, fouling out of the game is a *bad* thing. But there's a bigger picture here. I wanted to reward my son for fouling out. I wanted to bring blessings to him for his "bad" behavior. I know that might sound backward, and you might be thinking I'm unfit to be a parent, let alone a pastor.[3] But here's the thing: I knew that if Obadiah didn't learn how to play a more aggressive game of basketball, he wouldn't play past grade school. (He never did end up fouling out, but he came really close once!)

I bring all this up because the way God thinks about us and rewards us doesn't always match up with what we think he should do. He rewards things that we never would. Don't get me wrong, I'm not equating my attempt to get my son to be aggressive on the basketball court to the works of God. And I'm certainly not trying to make a moral equivalence there. What I'm observing is that we live in a culture that values things God doesn't value. And we live in a culture that

---

3   You're probably right; let's be real.

wants to embody a way of treating other people that is different from how God would. All of us are intuitively partaking in and learning from the ways people treat one another in this culture, whether we are followers of Jesus or not.

There is a bigger picture. And Jesus wants to keep Christianity weird. Now, I don't mean weird like the city across the river from where I live. They have signs that say Keep Portland Weird,[4] and they mean it! One time a pastor friend of mine came to town to speak at Crossroads, the church where I get the blessing of being the pastor. I remember he called me and said, "So, hey, I'm running late to our meeting. I got caught in traffic from the Portland's World Naked Bike Ride. Man, this is a crazy place!" So not weird like *that* kind of weird. But yes . . . weird.

This is where the "crazy" of crazy happy comes to the surface. The Beatitudes are an invitation to unlearn the cultural doctrines we've inherited and live into the beauty of God's kingdom. And, many times, that's just the opposite of the rules of the typical game, like in my basketball story. (Maybe just picture being more peaceable, not more violent, okay?)

This mixed-up, backward quality is happening in all our lives, every day. When you look at the past week of your life, there are probably many things of which you could say, "Yeah, so that's not really who I think I am. I've acted that way, but that's not my best self, my truest self. I wish you saw the real me."

We all intuitively know there is a gap between who we

---

[4]   I also know that Austin, Texas, uses the same slogan: Keep Austin Weird. And I'll refrain from making any jokes about Texas being weird.

hope we would be (or feel we really are) and the life we actually live out. And Jesus is inviting us once again not simply to *do* better but to embrace the beautiful reality of who we already are in him.

This "weird" way is the key to Christian happiness.

The Mercy Way

As we look at our next beatitude, we see Jesus's invitation to walk in mercy. This means both *forgiveness* for the guilty and *compassion* for those who are suffering.

I think the easiest way to understand mercy is through the lens of justice and grace. Here goes:

- Justice is getting what you deserve.
- Mercy is not getting what you deserve.
- Grace is getting what you don't deserve.

To use the example of Obadiah's basketball team again, justice is getting removed from the game because you fouled out. You got what you deserved. Five fouls and game over.

Mercy? You foul out, get removed from the game, and Dad takes you to dinner. You didn't get what you deserved.

Grace? You foul out of the game, Dad takes you out for dinner, and he gives you a trust fund.[5]

What's beautiful is that God is all of these: just, merciful, and gracious. God gives what we deserve. But the good news of Jesus Christ is that God gave the punishment that we de-

---

[5] Obadiah, if you are reading this, I am sorry but there is no trust fund, buddy. But I am hoping you become so wildly successful in life that I can be your smoothie-run guy.

served not to us but to Jesus. God is still just; it's part of his perfection.

God is also merciful, because sometimes he doesn't give us what we deserve. One of the most beautiful examples of mercy is the story of the prodigal son.

Jesus is quick to point out here that mercy is something we have received, and then we're also encouraged to extend mercy to other people. And we're not just talking about *feelings* of mercy. We're also talking about *concrete acts* of mercy—specific, practical things that move the needle.

So let's look at this idea with the whole picture in mind. The crazy happy life begins with our poverty of spirit, our awareness that we bring nothing to our relationship with God except our rebellion. That leads us to mourning for the ways we move in this world, producing meekness. That feeling of getting over ourselves then leads us to hunger and thirst for righteousness.

Now, part of God's righteousness is his mercy. Because we receive satisfaction from the goodness of God, we release our need to give people what we think they deserve. Talk about weird! Isn't that countercultural to the day and age in which we live?

But guess what? Justice is not the only attribute of God. God's way doesn't end with "an eye for an eye."[6] His way is different from our world's perspective of, "I want justice for my enemies, but I want mercy for me." We can identify with that, can't we? But that double standard within all of us grieves the heart of God.

We know from the book of Proverbs that having uneven

---

[6]   Matthew 5:38.

scales—judging things unfairly—is an abomination to God. He hates that. Because we have received mercy, Jesus expects us to extend it to others, regardless of what they "deserve." It's not our job to determine someone else's worthiness of mercy. And if you're anything like me, you can say, *Thank the Lord I'm not God,* right? Can I get an amen?

In Matthew 7:1–2, Jesus says, "Judge not, that you be not judged. For with what judgment you judge, you will be judged; and with the measure you use, it will be measured back to you."

Now, "Judge not" does not mean we walk around without any awareness or discernment. No, when Jesus used the word *judge* here, he was talking about condemnation—about closing the case as if you're the final voice on the matter.

Notice that, in one sense, God allows us to elect the criteria by which we are judged. He says, "However you judge other people is the way you will be judged." I don't know about you, but I've noticed I tend to be hardest on people who do the exact same things I do wrong. I get the most frustrated with people who sin in the same ways I do.

You want to know if you're really judgmental? If you think everybody else is judgmental, you probably are.

Paul said it this way in Galatians 6:7–10:

> Do not be deceived, God is not mocked; for whatever a man sows, that he will also reap. For he who sows to his flesh will of the flesh reap corruption, but he who sows to the Spirit will of the Spirit reap everlasting life. And let us not grow weary while doing good, for in due season we

shall reap if we do not lose heart. Therefore, as we
have opportunity, let us do good to all, especially
to those who are of the household of faith.

I love that Paul first said, "Don't think for a second that
God will be mocked. Whatever it is that you sow, you will
reap." Imagine if you were putting a garden together and you
planted a bunch of cucumbers; you wouldn't expect to harvest tomatoes from those cucumber seeds. Or, in this case,
you don't expect to plant tomatoes and end up with roses
instead. So when you sow to the flesh, you make an invest-
ment of planting seeds of rebellion against God. And, naturally, from the flesh, you will reap corruption. You will end
up with everything that is not fulfilling, let alone beautiful;
everything that is not healthy or holy; everything that is not
in your best interest or the best interest of anyone else. In
other words, we're talking about a rough situation.

But if you sow to the Spirit? You will of the Spirit reap
everlasting life. If you lock your life into the rhythms of God,
you're harvesting a beautiful life—one of, you guessed it,
crazy happiness.

What it comes down to is this: no one can make your
choices for you; what you do is up to you. And what's amazing is that God—as the true and living God, the all-knowing
one—doesn't make our choices for us either. He has allowed
each of us to make our own choices.

But you know what he does? He offers us his help, his
Spirit, to influence our decisions. The Spirit informs us of
God's perspective and reminds us how to get back there
when we're lost.

> What it comes down to is this: no one can make your choices for you; what you do is up to you.

If you've walked with Jesus for any length of time, you've experienced that, haven't you? You now have an unsettled feeling, a check in your spirit, when you rebel in ways you used to. It just doesn't feel *right* anymore. And at that juncture, you must choose what to do when that feeling of discomfort comes, when that conviction touches your life. Do you respond to it and flee temptation, or do you proceed on the course you're on?[7] Do you honor that check and flee youthful lusts and then turn to the Lord? Or do you walk away from the beautiful life? If you run to Jesus in that moment, that's how you reap everlasting life, which he defines as knowing himself.[8]

We are all farmers.[9] Every single day, every one of us is sowing. Every decision is sowing in either the flesh or the spirit. And it never stops. As long as you're here, as long as you have breath in your lungs, as long as you are making choices in life, you are sowing and reaping.

We all have to ask ourselves, *What kind of garden am I sowing right now?*

------

[7]   I like to call those moments the "God pause." As a follower of Jesus, often there's that moment right before you make a bad decision where you have that check, that conviction of the spirit, and then either obey or disobey.

[8]   See John 17:3.

[9]   We are farmers. Bum–da-bum–bum–bum–bum–bum. (Do you know that commercial?)

Don't Lose Heart

Here's something to keep in mind: you never get the harvest right away. Just as you sow your cucumber seeds, your tomato seeds, your apple tree seeds one day and don't expect to harvest the fruit in the next day (that's why Costco and Sam's Club exist, by the way), we may not see the harvest of what we're sowing today until a decade from now. Or two decades. Or more. And that's why the apostle Paul said, "Let us not grow weary while doing good, for in due season we shall reap if we do not lose heart."[10]

I want to talk about the times, on this journey with Jesus, when you're struggling to sow to the Spirit and you're feeling tired. And, man, is it hard to resist that one temptation or that lifestyle habit you've been doing for so long. And you're not getting what you want.

If you're right in the place where you're about to lose heart, where you've been doing your best for a long time and you've been grinding it out, I want to encourage you. Don't grow weary in doing good. Why? Because you're sowing good, and there's a promised reward for you. It's God's promise! Don't ever forget that. And as we talked about in chapter 5, that's why God is bearing the fruit of patience in our lives: so we can wait on him until it's time.

So if you're thinking, *I wish I had more love in my life; I wish I were receiving more love from other people,* guess what your job is? To love people more.

If you think the world should have more integrity (it should), you need to cultivate integrity in your own life. If you want to see more joy in the world, pray for God's joy to

---

10 Galatians 6:9.

absolutely invade your life. Do your best to bring heaps of joy to the room every time you walk in.

We give what we've received from God, and we receive what we give. That's why the merciful are blessed in the economy of God's kingdom. The merciful sow to the Spirit and reap day by day the things the Lord wants to pour out into the community around them.

You see that? That's powerful. Let's bring this full circle.

The fruit of the Spirit and the fruit of mercy is what? Kindness.

See how that all fits together? When we extend mercy to others because we've received it from God, we become known for our kindness. Kindness is nothing more, nor less, than the ability to behave toward others as God has behaved toward us. Kindness is pushing forward a winsomeness, a simple joyfulness, into all our relationships.

Many people who know me only as Pastor Daniel tell me I am such a kindhearted guy. But, to be totally honest, kindness is not something that comes at all naturally to me. Growing up in Jersey, in an all-Italian family, I've always been direct, sometimes way harsher than I've needed to be. I remember when Lynn and I first got married, she'd often say, "Daniel, kindness matters."

Originally, I blew the notion off. Not so much anymore. I have really taken it to heart.[11] I see now how much it matters. And my desires are changing as a result. When I think about the fact that God has shown greater mercy to me than I can imagine by sending Jesus to die in my place, it makes me

---

[11] I have been sufficiently housebroken. By the way, she may have just told me that again yesterday.

want to be merciful toward others. I'm a sinner, and God's been so good to me; you're a sinner like me, and God will be good to you like he has been to me. So, to the best of my still-imperfect abilities, I'm going to treat you with kindness.

Quite possibly the greatest need we have in this generation is for the people of God to become kind. To do so will mean that we are becoming more like who our Father is. So many people's primary impression of Christians is that they're unkind.

I remember when renowned theoretical physicist and cosmologist Stephen Hawking died. I was blown away (not in a good way) by so many Christians who simply *ragged* on this brilliant man. Yes, he was an atheist. Perhaps even anti-God. But what kind of witness do we show to a dying world when we take to pulpits and public forums only to share bitter and vengeful thoughts about other people? Even after their contributions to science? Even after they have died? I don't understand.

Here's the problem: we acted toward Stephen the way he acted toward believers, not the way Jesus acts toward us. I have to ask: Do we take our marching orders from the bitter leaders of the world, or from Jesus, the King of creation, who gave his life for us? Anytime we fall short of kindness, we fall short of the way of Jesus. We lose a little more of the crazy happiness that is meant to be ours.

We should never count the cost of kindness. It is not optional or an extra. It is simply our choosing to treat others the way God has treated us. This is what I like to call a "duh" moment. It's one of those situations where I say, *Duh, Fusco . . . there's nothing difficult about this one. Just show people the same kindness God showed you.*

I must clarify that I understand we can't control the caricatures of Christianity our culture sets up. When people want to make a point, others are all too easy to reduce and demonize. We see those memes every day on social media. But our responsibility is not to control an image; it is to represent Christ to the world. We can control how we witness to the work of Jesus within our spheres of influence, can't we? Of course! And this is where kindness changes everything.

The kindness of Jesus being on display in his bride, the church, is the first step toward healing the deep rifts between church and society. It's simple, really. When someone's been kind to you, even if you disagree on an issue, you'll listen because you love and trust that person. And so kindness wins us a witness. Kindness wins us the opportunity to be listened to when we share the good news of the gospel of Jesus Christ.

And if we mess this up, we've misrepresented Jesus in his world, because Jesus is absolutely, beyond the shadow of a doubt, the kindest person you'll ever meet. It's the goodness of the Lord that leads a person to repentance, and God's goodness is mediated through his people. (That is us, by the way.) The Cross tells of God's kindness and his mercy, but the church has to embody it in this world.

If God's unconditional love leads us into joy despite our circumstances, and that joy produces peace, which helps us walk in patience, then longsuffering makes us kind, because we know a good God is doing a good work.

And that's beautiful, isn't it? In his mercy, God wants to make us more kind. But that's not all. Take a look at a section in Paul's letter to Titus, in chapter 3, verses 1–2. What I love about this text is that it brings together, in a really powerful way, all these things we've been talking about. In these verses, Paul gives Titus a framework for how to treat others and how to instruct the congregation he served to live the same way: "to be subject to rulers and authorities, to obey, to be ready for every good work, to speak evil of no one, to be peaceable, gentle, showing all humility to all men." Now, isn't *that* a beautiful definition of kindness?

Paul reminds Titus that to live kindly in this world is all-encompassing. It determines how we relate to governing authorities, people we're in conflict with, our friends and acquaintances. And the crazy thing about kindness as Paul defines it is that it demands we treat all people equally: rulers and leaders, family members, and people we barely know or meet on the street. No matter who we are, we *all* receive the same measure of kindness in God's kingdom.

I'm sure you can imagine just how amazing living in a world governed by kindness would be. But for Paul, our kindness doesn't stand on its own. We can be truly kind only when we respond to the kindness of God extended to us.

Here's what I mean. Paul follows his definition of kindness this way in verses 3–8:

> We ourselves were also once foolish, disobedient, deceived, serving various lusts and pleasures, living in malice and envy, hateful and hating one another. But when the kindness and the love of God our Savior toward man appeared, not by works of righteousness which we have done, but according to His mercy He saved us, through the washing of regeneration and renewing of the Holy Spirit, whom He poured out on us abundantly through Jesus Christ our Savior, that having been justified

by His grace we should become heirs according to the hope of eternal life.

This is a faithful saying, and these things I want you to affirm constantly, that those who have believed in God should be careful to maintain good works. These things are good and profitable to men.

Do you see how the apostle Paul brings mercy and kindness and everything we've been talking about all together? Basically, he said, "And now I want to make sure you guys are living it out loud."

What do I mean by living it out loud? I'm so glad you asked.

Paul started off with this instruction to be kind. Then he said to Titus, "Remember, you weren't always like this. You were all messed up. You were dead in the eyes of the living God." But then he hit us with the glory of verse 4: "The kindness and the love of God our Savior toward man appeared." And then he made this qualification: "Not by our works of righteousness, but according to God's own mercy he saved us."[12]

Our washing and regeneration, our renewing by the Holy Spirit, who God poured out on us abundantly through Jesus Christ our Savior—that's how we've literally been brought from death to life. Walking out kindness is part of walking in the life we've already received from Christ. It's part of truly living.

The beautiful life *is* true life. The beautiful life fulfills our

---

[12] Author's paraphrase of verse 5.

deepest longings. That's why I love to say that Jesus is real—not only because he is alive[13] but because everything that is true reality is found in him. Everything else is only an illusion.

I've said it before: what God sees as beautiful isn't what we do but who we are. The crazy happy life is Christ in us. There's no such thing as life apart from God, but many of us spend too much time living as though our lives are our own.

When we realize the incredible kindness of God in sending Jesus—when we understand the mercy of God, that Jesus took our place—we live in this world as people who are well aware that they've received the greatest gift. As followers of Jesus, we bear the responsibility to be vehicles of God's kindness and mercy in a world that's screaming for justice. Because God has been merciful to us, we can add mercy back into a society pulled between a desperate longing not to be judged and a subversively intense judgment of any set of values that doesn't match today's cultural norms.

Our part in making sure God's mercy reigns in this generation is not to get angry. No, instead of being rabidly angry, we are to be kind like our Savior is kind. Once again, Jesus turns everything on its head and says to do the opposite of what the culture is telling us. God's view of beauty is unique.

Who was ever saved because Christians were mean? That never raises the spiritual temperature of anybody's heart. You probably know this, but, actually, a harsh and mean Christian voice makes people more repulsed by the good news that God would send Jesus. They think God is an evil

---

[13] And he absolutely is alive!

judge. But when God's mercy drives us to kindness, we become the fragrance of the life of Jesus to a dying world.

So whether you've been walking with Jesus a long time or this is a new journey for you, don't ever let other people define your understanding of what kindness and mercy is; let Jesus. Because deep down, we're all hoping God is as good and as kind and as merciful as he says he is. And the truth is, my friends, God is *exactly* who he says he is! So when we live into the reality of who he says we are, well, that's when we live the life God calls beautiful.

And with kindness upon kindness, we'll be blessed.

Crazy blessed.

Crazy happy blessed.

7

The Crazy Happy Way of Goodness

Blessed are the pure in heart,
For they shall see God.

—Matthew 5:8

The fruit of the Spirit is . . . goodness.

—Galatians 5:22

Family road trips are something else.

Every couple of years, my parents rented a place in Florida,[1] and we'd all go to Disney World. My dad always really wanted to get from our home in New Jersey to Florida via the Blue Ridge Parkway, a route he'd romanticized for a long time because it took you straight through the picture-perfect Blue Ridge Mountains. Of course, none of the rest of

---

[1] To get from New Jersey to Florida, it felt as though we drove through about ninety-seven states in the span of twelve hours. As a grown adult, I live on the West Coast, and it would take me twelve hours just to drive from the Washington-Oregon border south to California. And yes, I know America is made up of only fifty states. It's hyperbole, okay?

us were interested in mountains at the time, so we always whined when my dad tried to convince us that we should take that route. Usually we got our way—until one year, when it finally clicked for him that there was only one steering wheel in the car. I distinctly recall the day he finally won the annual family argument by default with the insurmountable argument, "Too bad. I'm driving." No arguing with that.

So we went. As it turns out, the Blue Ridge Parkway is stunning. Picture being in one of the only cars on a highway that twists through mile after mile of foothills. Stately trees spread in every direction. The sky above is an expanse of blue that melts into a horizon smeared with vivid green and deep yellow, punctuated by the occasional patch of bright-pink rhododendrons. In the mornings, the sun rises violet and indigo and sets in amber and tangerine. It's glorious.

No wonder my dad was dying to enjoy this drive! But did we let him? No, of course not. My two sisters and I were, unfortunately, your classic road-trip killers that year. "Are we there yet? When will it be over? Is there a McDonald's coming up?"

I'll never forget looking up from the back seat and seeing my dad shake his head in shame and disappointment. All he'd wanted to do for so long was revel in these mountains, and he didn't get a chance to enjoy them.

I understand it better now. As a parent, I find this happens to me all the time with my own children. Kids are just kids. They have a hard time being patient.[2] So often, Lynn tells our kids, "We're going somewhere beautiful." And the kids

---

[2]   In the previous chapter, we spoke about reaping what we sow. Ugh!

are like, "This is boring!"[3] And to some extent, that's normal kid behavior. Still, had I known then what I know now, I would have tried to enjoy the beauty of that moment with my dad.

Reflecting on that experience recently has reminded me that, in some ways, you're going to see what you want to see in life.

It doesn't take a huge leap in logic to see this principle in play all over our culture. Two people can look at the exact same situation or idea but *see* radically different things in it. If you don't believe me, just read the reviews posted online for any movie or restaurant. For one, what they see is the most mind-blowing, beautiful experience. For another, it's the most tragic experience. And the difference comes from what it is that you bring to the table.

We've been looking at the crazy happiness of what Jesus taught. As we live into that beautiful, upside-down life, we become truly fulfilled. (Just not in the way we expect.) And each day, we are cultivating that whether we are aware of it or not. And we're going to see in both the Beatitudes and the fruit of the Spirit that exact same idea: in a lot of ways, your life will be what you want it to be and not anything more or less than that.[4]

---

[3] I'll never forget when we brought our kids to one of my favorite places in the world, Crater Lake in southern Oregon. A six-year-old Obadiah popped out of the car, looked at the lake surrounded by snowcapped mountains, and said, "Is that it?"

[4] Okay, we all know that Madonna was right about one thing: "We are living in a material world, and I am a material girl." But when I say your life is what you make it to be, I don't mean materially. I don't mean we always get what we want in life, because "you can't always get what you

If you want your life to be an amazing experience, it will be, because you're going to look at everything with a sense of awe and wonder that transforms even your most mundane moments. If you've decided that life is going to be lame and a grind, it's probably going to be. If you decide that your spouse is the worst person ever, then guess what? You're going to see your spouse as the worst person, even if he or she is not. And if you've decided to give your spouse the benefit of the doubt when you disagree, then even though neither of you is perfect, you're going to be okay.

I realize this probably sounds radical, but stick with me. God allows each one of us to bring the same thing into every situation, and that "thing" is ourselves. And the way we walk with Jesus in the day in and the day out largely determines our experience for every situation.[5] If you're looking for fault, you're going to find it.

I'm not saying it's all in your head. Obviously, tragedy strikes. Some days are objectively better than others. But the apostle Paul (no stranger to *really* bad days) said that he learned how to be content regardless of his circumstances. Talk about the power of our mindset in Jesus!

---

want." (Okay, I'll stop quoting lyrics.) I do mean that much of life is determined by our perspective. We are the only common denominator in every situation we encounter.

[5]   Of course, this is not true for situations outside your control. More specifically, abuse and trauma are total exceptions to what I'm getting at here. If you've been victimized by someone else, that is not your fault, and we all need help healing from the wounds dealt to us by other people. I'm only speaking of the normal daily life circumstances most every human being experiences and how our responsibility is to walk with Jesus in each of those things, submitting both our actions and our perspectives to his holy oversight.

As we've gone through this journey with Jesus so far in the book, I've said that we're examining a life Jesus lays out for us in the *Beatitudes*, not the *Do*-attitudes. He's not asking us to do more but to more fully live into who he's already called and crafted us to be. At the same time, Jesus reminds us that our job is to *own* our lives: who we are, what we see, what we bring into each situation.

Every way in which we choose to live and love is a communicable disease.

Owning your life as you walk with the Lord is important. Why? Because when you're walking with Jesus, you will influence other people. In fact, every way in which we choose to live and love is a communicable disease. Grumpiness is a communicable disease. So is joyfulness.[6] What we bring into our interactions with others ripples out into the world around us. The mysterious and beautiful nature of God's world is that we live in an entirely *relational* ecosystem. Everything I do affects you. Everything you do affects me.

Pure Mercy

In our journey through the characteristics of a beautiful life, we left off with Jesus promising blessing for those who are merciful—those who don't treat others the way they deserve

---

[6]   The big question for each of us is, "What disease am I spreading?" It's a strange but important question.

to be treated. And he very naturally rolls into what we're looking at next: "Blessed are the pure in heart."

Maybe it's easy for you to see how mercy and a pure heart might depend on each other. But if you're like me, purity of heart is something that makes you do a double take, no matter where you see it. I'm fairly aware of the motives of my own heart, and let me tell you, even when I'm doing the right thing, my heart is not always in the right place. A pure heart? Seems like a pretty tall order to me—like something only God could do. (You see where this is going, right?)

The good news is, even though we have to own our choices and take responsibility for our lives, it's not up to us to *create* pure hearts for ourselves. We do bear responsibility for one thing though: we need to *let* Jesus purify us. And he gives us a specific *location* for that work of purification he wants to unfold in our lives. Did you catch that? "Blessed are the pure in *heart*." This is huge.

Here's why. When Jesus originally preached his Sermon on the Mount, he was speaking to a crowd primarily composed of two distinct groups of people: the common folk, who characteristically saw who Jesus was and celebrated, and the religious leaders, who didn't see who Jesus was. And, more specifically, they definitely didn't *want* to see who Jesus was.

Here's the interesting thing: Jesus's teaching here about the heart was probably targeted to the second group. Often Jesus cleverly targeted comments and questions to the religious leaders to surface what was really going on in *their* hearts, as they were usually most concerned with *external* purity. They were very focused on making sure they said the right things and dressed the right way and knew the right people. They fulfilled the minutiae of the Mosaic law in very specific ways that would be acceptable to people just like them. They performed elaborate ceremonies to purify their bodies. In other words, they *looked* really good.[7]

So it's no coincidence that Jesus gets at heart-level purity here. He's *intentionally* giving the crowds an impossible order: purify what can't be touched by ceremonial bathing or strict adherence to a diet. Purify your *hearts*. This is an absolutely impossible order. The crowds Jesus spoke to would have known that as well as we do.

Purity of heart doesn't mean we just get rid of all the plaque and buildup in our arteries.[8] The heart is the control center of life. In the Hebrew, the word for "heart" is the same word for "bowels."[9] But the image in the Hebrew language is that our hearts encompass the deepest parts of who we are. So the heart houses our thoughts and our emotions and our desires and our temptations. With our hearts, we listen for the still, small voice[10] of the Holy Spirit.

Jesus specifically gives this blessing, but with criteria that's impossible for us to meet. Why? Because he wants us to trust *him* to do the work that would be impossible otherwise. Jesus isn't satisfied with just cleaning up the front yard, making a life presentable for the neighbors. No, he wants to clean

---

[7] I don't think they were like this on purpose. They didn't realize the error of their ways. But Jesus called them out a bunch about this type of hypocrisy.

[8] You have to admit that's a pretty witty turn of the idea. But it would be a great thing to have no blockage to the heart.

[9] Yeah, I know it's kind of awkward to think about it.

[10] 1 Kings 19:12.

house. He wants to bring *real* purity, not just the appearance. Jesus knows that if he gets the inside right, everything on the outside of our lives will begin to change too.

In our self-help-obsessed culture, Jesus is *radical* in his commitment to real change. Radically different. Now, I'm not actually against self-help, as the opposite would be self-hurt or self-neglect, neither of which is good.

The problem with contemporary self-help is that it tries to get you to the right place in a way that will never actually get you there. Self-help often reveals the right destination, but the only way to actually get there is through Jesus. No matter what work you do, even if you see some growth in various areas of your life, the essential purification of the control center of your life is never accomplished by dealing with external things. The purification of our hearts is only ever a work of God, and it's all-encompassing.

Here is one of the great secrets of the crazy happy life: in every detail of our lives, in every seemingly insignificant moment, God is seeking to purify us.

Pure Presence

Let's face it: life is not all just a lovely drive to Florida. Reality isn't like that. Unfortunately, "every detail" includes suffering. Actually, one of God's *greatest* ways of purifying our lives is through suffering. Now, don't get me wrong; I'm just like you when I hear that. Nobody likes suffering or going through hard times.

But often we add to our difficulty by thinking that we must have done something wrong when things get tough. But that's hardly ever true. Suffering, for righteous people, isn't punishment. (Just read the book of Job!). It's for purification.

God loves when we're honest with him about our grief; he doesn't expect us to just suck it up and white-knuckle our way through the difficulties of life. But when we trust who he is, we can choose to submit ourselves to his work, and that's when Jesus bears fruit in our lives not just in spite of our suffering but because of it.

Think about the gym. People get up too early to go work too hard (while wearing goofy clothes) in a whole room full of sweaty people. And they pay good money to do it![11] And the rest of us who aren't working out are thinking, *I should be working out, but I'm not.* We know we'd be healthier if we exercised. We all intuitively (and scientifically, at this point) know that if we force our bodies out of their comfort zones, sure, we'll get sore, but we'll build muscle and be healthier in the long run. What's the point? Well, in the big scheme of things, no pain, no gain.

I don't want to oversimplify this. I trust you to hear what I'm saying and not take this to some extreme, like thinking every hangnail is meant to sanctify you. But don't mistake me either. Don't ever think that God hasn't woven spiritual principles into the physical world. Suffering—emotional and spiritual pain—is a catalyst for endurance and strength, growth that we otherwise wouldn't come by. The one whom God loves, God disciplines.

That's why in the Bible, you'll often see the imagery of refining metal as a representation of our own purification. As a precious metal heats up, it becomes soft enough for the impurities within to rise to the surface, where they can be

---

[11] I personally prefer my home gym. Plus, a picture of me in my workout headband might break the internet.

scraped off. Then the cooling metal can be shaped into something even lovelier than what it was previously. God does the same thing with our hearts.

Don't miss the fact that if a refiner turns the heat up too much, it actually *destroys* the metal. But without adequate heat, there's no purifying effect on the metal. Every situation in your life—the money troubles, the relationship struggles, the loneliness, the fear, the anxiety, the issues with your family, the drama with your friends, all the ways the five-year plan is working out and isn't—is God's way of turning the heat up in your life so that your hardness of heart will soften and impurities will come to the surface and he can purify and remake your heart to be more beautiful than before.

Can you see how it's a no-brainer to Jesus that this information would change the way we look at our lives? Hear this paraphrase of Matthew 5:8: "Oh how happy are those who've had their hearts purified by God! Oh, how fortunate is the person who God loves enough to use suffering to surface all the garbage in his or her heart to be redeemed!"

That changes everything, my friends. Armed with this information, when things hurt us, we can still trust that God is good and is working through everything in our lives to make us pure.

Purity of heart brings us not only into our own beauty in a new way but into the Lord's beauty too. Check out Psalm 24:3–6:

> Who may ascend into the hill of the LORD?
> Or who may stand in His holy place?
> He who has clean hands and a pure heart,

Who has not lifted up his soul to an idol,
Nor sworn deceitfully.
He shall receive blessing from the LORD,
And righteousness from the God of his salvation.
This is Jacob, the generation of those who seek Him,
Who seek Your face.

The psalmist asks something we all wonder at some point: Who is allowed to stand in the presence of God? The one who has clean hands and a pure heart, the one in whom God has done a work of purification, may stand before the Lord. And God is inviting each one of us to be a part of his joy and purity no matter what pain and sorrow and sin we've endured or created.

Part of the beautiful life Jesus invites us to and desires for us depends on our willingness to bring our messiest and hardest moments to him, trusting him to leverage the nasty stuff to bring something beautiful out of it.

You know the saying: life will make us bitter or it will make us better. It all depends on how we encounter it. Our response to our circumstances will either draw us closer to Jesus, who will make us better, or pull us away from Jesus, where we grow bitter.

You Will See God

Jesus promises the pure in heart that they will *see* God. When Jesus purifies our hearts, that internal work radically affects every other part of our lives, too, and in Matthew 5:8, Jesus specifically takes a look at our eyes, representing our perspective on things.

Purity of heart gives us "eyes" that "see" clearly. Purity of heart transforms our perspective on everything so that in every situation we encounter, we have the ability to discern who God is, what he's done, and what he's doing—not only for ourselves but for other people as well.

Purity of heart gives us *vision*. But any point of view is a view from a point. Two people seeing the exact same thing will see two different things. Purity of heart is the difference between those of us who are convinced Jesus is real and others of us who are not convinced at all.

When you allow God to purify your heart, you begin to see the Lord's hand in everything. We become like King David in Psalm 27:13 when he says, "I would have lost heart, unless I had believed that I would see the goodness of the LORD in the land of the living."

But the wild thing is that we can fight growth. We can hold ourselves back by being unwilling to experience hard things. If I decide, *I will not allow God to leverage my life to purify me,* I will see only what I want to see. And that's likely to be quite different from reality. Just as Jesus said, "Out of the abundance of the heart the mouth speaks,"[12] so, too, out of the abundance of the heart *the eyes see.*

That's God's end goal, his *telos,*[13] as he purifies our hearts. That's his ultimate purpose in our suffering, that it will lead to purification with the result that you and I will learn how to see God—in our circumstances, in our trials, in what goes wrong, in what goes right, in the victories and the defeats.

---

[12]   Matthew 12:34.

[13]   I just had to drop a Greek word there so you would know that I am smart like that.

We begin to see the Lord's hand not only in the acceptances but also in the rejections.[14] We begin to see that our present reality, right here and now, is ultimately a work of a good God who loves us too much to leave us the way he finds us. And that changes the way we see *everything*.

It's not difficult to look at our world and see only the depravity and brokenness. I get the same news feeds as you, so I know how easy it can be to see the bad stuff. But, believe it or not, the idea of a Christian being negative is antibiblical.

Negativity comes quickly in a culture of outrage. It is probably fair to say that it is the natural outcome of it. But when Jesus is purifying your heart, and God is showing you himself in the midst of the world, all you have to bring to any given situation is hope. Because God is not done with you yet. Or your loved ones. Or the world. And when we lean into him, he brokers that hope to us.

A pastor I work with used to be in real-estate sales. He'd place hundreds of cold calls every day to talk to people about real estate. Most of the time, people would yell at him, ask how he got their names, or just hang up. Now that he's a pastor, he still calls people. But these calls are different: he's reaching out to ask if they need prayer or want to talk more about Jesus. When he calls people to talk with them about Jesus, it's totally different. He told me, "Pastor Daniel, I love making those calls. It was one thing to be a real-estate broker, but now I'm a hope broker."[15]

I love that description. We're *all* supposed to be hope brokers! God wants us to be people of tremendous hope. This

---

[14]   Remember that rejection is God's protection.

[15]   Preach it, Pastor Robby.

doesn't mean pretending the world isn't broken. It means trusting that God is remaking this world in his name through Jesus. It means trusting (sometimes this is so hard) that God is doing a work in you so that you can be a vehicle for his goodness to enter the world.

Seeing a New World

Not only does purity of heart give us eyes to see *God* in the midst of our circumstances, but we begin to see the *world* through a new lens too. When Jesus watched the crowds of people who came to hear him teach, he knew the deceptiveness of their hearts. He was one with the Father, and he always saw people accurately. But he never stood in condemnation over them. He was always moved with compassion on behalf of everyone he met. Even when he hung on the cross, he cried out, "Father, forgive them, for they do not know what they are doing."[16]

Do you ever notice in the Bible that when the Lord calls somebody, he never seems to call them because they're so awesome? I mean, Gideon was hiding out in a cave, totally freaked out, when God called him. David was just a boy tending his father's flocks when Samuel anointed him king of Israel.

God sees something in people we don't. He sees things in us that we don't. Hear me clearly there: God sees beauty in you that you can't see yet. When God gives us eyes to see him, he also gives us eyes to see other people. And we don't just see people based on what they are; we see them with the potential that God sees in them. He wants to call out beauty in

---

[16] Luke 23:34 (NIV).

others, through us, through the vision he allows us to have for the lives of others. We participate in making the new world God intends as our perceptions change through the purification of our hearts.

Let's get practical. Each of us knows a person who needs God's love. Maybe it's a coworker. Maybe a family member. Maybe a neighbor. Maybe it's someone whose life is, to borrow a phrase, all jacked up. Maybe it's someone whose life is working exactly the way she wants it to but she doesn't know Jesus yet.

And this brings us to the next fruit of the Spirit. As we examine the list of fruits next to what Jesus has been teaching us in the Beatitudes, we find this: the fruit of purity is goodness.

By and large, the word *goodness* means "generosity."[17] God has created each one of us to be vehicles for his goodness to enter the world. But what usually comes to mind for us first here is *material* generosity. As human beings, that's often where our focus lands first: on the "stuff" we can give away. But that's only one facet of generosity. See, anytime you go out of your way to help somebody, to give and do good, you are being generous.

Jesus said his Father demonstrated this generous goodness: "My Father makes the rain fall on the just and on the unjust."[18] He's talking about God's amazing generosity. God doesn't just provide for people who are "good"; he takes care of *everyone*! The idea of us walking in goodness is that at

---

[17] Dictionary.com, s.v. "goodness," accessed February 13, 2020, dictionary.com/browse/goodness.

[18] See Matthew 5:45.

every point in our lives, we do our best to be a vehicle for God's generosity to enter the world.

Jesus lived this goodness—this generous life—all the time. Even in situations in which the religious people of his day were merciless and cold. When he was asked to harshly judge a woman who had been caught in the very act of adultery, he protected her, even though in the Jewish culture of the time, she could have been killed for her actions. Jesus not only showed mercy to the woman but also *advocated* for her (and notice the conspicuous absence of the man who should have been deemed equally guilty as she). Jesus hates injustice, so he generously extended mercy to her.[19]

And I love this example: Jesus told the story of the Pharisee and the tax collector, both praying in the temple courts. The Pharisee prayed in judgment over the publican, but the publican humbly repented before God. And Jesus said, "Yeah, that publican? *He's* the one who went away justified."[20] Jesus had a good and generous heart.

God is not content for our faith to remain in our heads. He's not content for our faith to just remain in the Bible either. God places his Word through the Bible into our heads, hoping it's going to make that (sometimes hard) eighteen-inch journey to our hearts and then out to our hands and our feet and back up to our mouths and our minds. Does that journey of the truth make sense? His way is to let rich life flow through us and out, just like it flows from him.

People should know that Jesus is real by watching how we

---

[19] See John 8:1–12.

[20] See Luke 18:9–14.

live. Most people are not going to start their journeys of faith by picking up the Bible on their own. They're going to read the living epistle of your life. That's why it's absolutely crucial that we live as vehicles of God's generosity and goodness to all. If they don't vote the way we vote, that doesn't mean we shouldn't be good to them. If they root for opposing sports teams, Jesus still calls us to be good to them. If they don't believe what we believe . . .

I think you get the idea.

We're supposed to be generous like God is, letting our goodness rain down on the just, the unjust, and everyone in between. The standard by which we determine if we should be good to someone else is not how similar we are; it's our shared humanity. Simply based on the fact that other people are human beings made in the image of God (just like us), we need to live generously toward them. If others are in need—of money, of attention, of kindness, of loving truth—it doesn't matter if they're different from us in some way. We take care of them.

Why? Because our faith in Jesus is the ultimate source of identity. Brothers and sisters, listen.

You are in Christ, first and foremost. You are *Christian* above all. Everything else falls way down the list. You may love your country, but guess what? Your first allegiance is to Jesus. You can hold your politics passionately, but you're a follower of Jesus first.[21] Think of all the other dividing lines

---

[21] While we're on this topic, let me just say this: whatever your views are on all the divisive things of our day (sexuality, politics, reality TV, chicken sandwiches, and so on), any view that doesn't account for your first loyalty being to Jesus is flawed and really dangerous. Only when we

we draw: income, race, education, interests, gender. They are all a far second to your identity in Christ (or at least they should be).

It seems like a lot of pressure, but this is the truth: when people think of Jesus, they're going to think of you. And when they think of you, let them think of the goodness of God on display.

Your purity of heart leads to goodness toward others. The crazy happy life is full of goodness. We amplify the goodness present and inaugurate it when it is absent, no matter where we are.

And then, as we live as God's people moving in the world in the name of Jesus as vehicles of his goodness, we shine forth a love that is unstoppable. And that's something that's beautiful to everyone, even a dying world.

Don't miss the fact that when people experience goodness, they become happy. That happiness causes them to walk in more goodness. No, it's not the crazy happiness we have been discussing. But it is the seed that could grow into it.

I think we would all agree that this world needs more goodness. Let's allow our crazy happy lives to supply it.

---

live in that rightful prioritization can we become vehicles of God's goodness. Our culture tries to reduce the categories of people who "deserve" our kindness and care. God wants us to do good to all.

8

The Crazy Happy Way of Faithfulness

Blessed are the peacemakers,
For they shall be called sons of God.
—Matthew 5:9

The fruit of the Spirit is . . . faithfulness.
—Galatians 5:22

Before we really begin this chapter, I want to hit "pause" for a moment. Let's make sure we're all on the same page about something.

Each of us lives our own life. We want our lives to reflect the things we value most. There's nothing more frustrating than knowing the person that you want to be, that you're *striving* to be, and not seeing that person. As we move toward the beautiful life of crazy happiness, we begin to bridge that gap between the person we want to be (and who God wants us to be) and the person we are now. Jesus redeemed humanity so we could experience his beautiful life down to the grittiest details of who we are. That's a process.

As we explore the Beatitudes and the fruit of the Spirit, we find that God wants our belief to hit street level in our lives. He wants to actually transform the way we live. Talk isn't enough.

But I need to stress that this is not just a legalistic demand to appease God; it blesses us in the process. What's wonderful is that obedience to God, in its own way, builds a full and abundant life for us.[1]

Not long ago, someone said to me, "Pastor Daniel, when I hear you speak, you're always talking about the *invitations* of God, but you don't actually talk about the *commandments* of God." I took that comment to heart. After I thought more about it, I went back to the person and said, "Well, actually, the commandments of God *are* invitations."

God could just tell us what life is supposed to be, and it could stop right there. But that's not how he works. God doesn't just "talk at" us. When God speaks, his words are invitations to good things, invitations to which we each need to respond. *Is what God says changing the way I live?* That's the real question. We each have to ask it honestly.

As a pastor and Bible teacher, if I'm going to teach something, I actually want to be living it first.[2] I'm in the habit, at this point, of asking the Lord for opportunities to live the messages that I get to share before I share them. And let me tell you, the Lord *always* answers that prayer. Sometimes it's

---

[1] Please do not think that I am speaking materially here. It's tragic how the good news of Jesus has been co-opted to be seen through the lens of wealth, greed, and materialism. The abundant life focuses on eternal things, not temporary pleasures.

[2] I don't want to be *that guy*, you know? That guy who talks the talk and doesn't walk the walk.

funny, sometimes it's convicting, and sometimes it happens when I screw something up and have to fix things.

Funnily enough, not long ago I had a *great* opportunity to live out, in my own family, Jesus's teaching about being a peacemaker. Except I wasn't the one making peace; I actually totally failed. But Lynn was a peacemaking all-star.

The memory is still vividly imprinted in my mind. Our kids were out of school on spring break, so we hopped on a plane and flew to California's Bay Area to visit family and take a needed vacation.

Everything was perfectly planned for the whole week, right up to the early Saturday-morning return flight—you know, so I could get back in time to rest for the evening and then preach on Sunday at Crossroads.

Now, I'm notorious for running late to everything,[3] but we had little kids, so it's not like anyone was sleeping in the hotel room anyway. Naturally, we got to the airport in plenty of time. Obadiah, Maranatha, Annabelle, and I all got through security super fast because we were able to use my TSA PreCheck. But for some reason, only Lynn's boarding pass wasn't designated for the PreCheck. No matter how much I tried to schmooze them, the security agents wouldn't let Lynn through the PreCheck line. Then we noticed that the security line that Lynn was in wasn't moving. At all.

I was standing there sweating and praying as though I could will the line into moving faster, but sure enough, fifteen minutes . . . thirty-five minutes . . . an hour—Lynn still wasn't through security. Then I heard the dreaded words: "Final boarding, Portland, Oregon." My kids and I took off

---

[3]   I'm on Italian time, remember?

running for the gate because I thought maybe I could convince the flight attendants to keep it open.[4]

Looking back, I laugh because you could totally see everyone's personalities coming out in that run through the airport. Maranatha, who's both awesome and a perfectionist,
was upset because we were running late. Obadiah, being the
oldest, just had to win the race to the gate. Annabelle, our
youngest, would run all day long, unless you *ask* her to run,
and then she no longer wants to. So, of course, that happened.

And then as we arrived at the gate huffing and puffing,
Maranatha had the startling conclusion that we were leaving
Mommy behind, and she got very upset until I convinced her
I would never leave Mommy behind.

But you might know what customer service is like with
certain airline carriers: not good.[5] I tried every argument I
could think of. I had three kids with me, for pity's sake, and
the two girls were crying! "If we don't get this flight, we're
going to be in the airport all day, and everyone's going to
have a terrible airport experience because my kids are crazy.
Can you just hold it for *five minutes*?" But to everything,
they said no.

Five minutes later, Lynn sprinted up to the gate—right
after they had officially closed the door. Then the kids had to

---

[4]   I can't fathom that after my failure with the security agents, I didn't
realize that my Jedi mind-trick skills were nonoperative at this moment.

[5]   It's taking a *lot* of self-control not to call out the airline by name right
now. But even though we haven't gotten to that fruit of the Spirit yet, I'm
still going to live it out!

be comforted, and we had to figure out an alternate flight. I just sat down and closed my mouth, overwhelmed and stressed out.[6]

Then I looked over at Lynn. She smiled. "God's got a good plan," she said. Because I can still be so childish, I rolled my eyes. (Not proud of it.) And I may or may not have acted like I was gagging too.[7]

Because she's the best person I know,[8] Lynn ignored my childishness and just said, "Daniel, there's a million reasons why we had to miss that flight."

Of course, everything worked out logistically. We got a rental car, enjoyed the extra time we suddenly had, and would still get back in time for church the next day. But I won't lie. I was grumpy all day because it wasn't *my* plan that worked out. I wanted to get home. I wanted to get back to our routine before work started. I had hoped to catch a nap (vacation can really take it out of a guy). Even though everything worked out, I felt justified in staying grumpy.

The day passed. Finally, when we were driving back to the airport to get on our later flight, Lynn said, "You know what, Daniel? You know what I think really happened? I think there were other people who needed to be home because maybe there's something going on in their families and they needed our seats more than we did."

I was so convicted. Whether that was the case or not, my

---

[6] To my credit, I am just grateful that Jesus is transforming me. Me closing my mouth is serious progress.

[7] Lynn always tells me that I have loud body language.

[8] Next to Jesus, of course.

wife had the right perspective. I was just acting like a grump.[9] What I realized was that even though I love Jesus and I'm a pastor, I was still not living into my life in Jesus as I know I should. I was allowing my own disappointment to cloud my perspective. But Lynn was letting the peace of God rule her heart throughout the whole thing.

It hit me a little later that I had the most amazing opportunity to be a peacemaker within my family but didn't lean into that opportunity. I pushed it away because my agenda was leading the way. When I look back on it now, I am sure that wasn't my finest hour. And it definitely wasn't me living crazy happy either. However, my wife in that moment was a *textbook* peacemaker. I was hot under the collar about my spoiled plans, but Lynn had the right vision of the situation. Whatever the reason for our missed flight was, it was bigger than our preferences. We had to remember that.

Not only did Lynn make peace in our family with that well-timed word, but she gave our kids a whole new perspective on inconvenience. She taught us all what it really looks like when you value other people above yourself. Because of that, everything else changed for the better.

Lynn is a great example to me (and now you too) of what Jesus means when he says, "Blessed—crazy happy, fortunate, highly favored—are the peacemakers."

Blessed Are the *Who*?

The peacemakers—these amazing people who find ways to *make* peace. In a world characterized by conflict, outrage,

---

[9]   Or as my kids like to say, I was . . . (wait for it) . . . Grumpelstiltskin.

and rivalry, peacemakers are those who proactively seek to fix what is broken. No wonder they're blessed!

Before we dig into them, notice something with me. Jesus *doesn't* say, "Blessed are the *peaceful*." Peacemakers aren't docile and compliant. Peacemakers are not passive. No, peacemakers are actually proactive in the midst of conflict and rivalry and discord. Peacemakers are proactive at fixing things. They are the literal injection of God's peace into situations full of conflict.

The word *peace* as Jesus used it is related to the Hebrew word *shalom* (which you may remember from chapter 4). Theologian Cornelius Plantinga wrote the best definition of shalom I've ever found:

> The webbing together of God, humans, and all creation in justice, fulfillment, and delight is what the Hebrew prophets call *shalom*. We call it peace, but it means far more than mere peace of mind or a cease-fire between enemies. In the Bible, shalom means *universal flourishing, wholeness, and delight*—a rich state of affairs in which natural needs are satisfied and natural gifts fruitfully employed.[10]

In other words, shalom is the way things ought to be. Yeah. *Wow.*

We often think of a peacemaker as somebody who tries to

---

[10] Cornelius Plantinga Jr., *Not the Way It's Supposed to Be: A Breviary of Sin* (Grand Rapids, MI: Eerdmans, 1995), 10.

help when things are broken, or somebody who has that sweet Yoda-like calm.[11] But in the Bible, peacemaking is about something totally different. A peacemaker is a follower of Jesus who lives, inspired by the Holy Spirit, to remake the world into what it ought to be.

Let's put this in the framework of the rest of the Beatitudes. We should have the flow pretty much memorized by now. Our poverty of spirit produces in us a soft, breakable heart, and we find ourselves mourning our brokenness and the brokenness of the world. Mourning leads us to meekness, where we're over ourselves. Meekness moves us right into hungering and thirsting for God's righteousness, and Jesus promises to satisfy us. Our longing for the righteous ways of God forms in us merciful hearts and pure hearts, where we see the world and other people through the compassionate eyes of Jesus. And that inspires us to be makers of peace—people who carry God's shalom to a broken world.

I know that might sound freaky for many of us—freaky as in *discouraging*. That kind of reality is so far from where we live right now, isn't it? But here's the thing: there's *never* been a generation that has experienced shalom like I just explained. Sorry to pop your bubble. The only truly peaceful generation was the first one, I guess, all the way back to Adam and Eve in the garden, before they ate of the tree of the knowledge of good and evil.

Poet John Milton called it paradise lost. But one of the best parts of the story of Jesus is paradise being reclaimed, the original shalom reacquired through his redemption.

---

[11] Or someone sitting legs crossed, eyes closed, chanting, "*Ommmmmmm.*"

What God is looking for in every generation is our willingness to join him in that—to become proactive makers of peace as we respond in faith to Jesus, and to look at the missed flight of this world and think, *There must be something bigger going on here. How can I help?*

All things working together the way they should, universal flourishing on this side of eternity—that's what God has redeemed us for. But that's a scary proposition for many people today. We have become too comfortable in this world—the security of our lifestyles and the cushiness of our preferences. We're often caught hiding behind our technology as a substitute for real relationships, and when conflict comes along, we are reluctant to engage. But the people of God were designed to bring peace to the world, especially within their relationships, their sphere of influence.

This is important. So often in church, we hear about Jesus's death and resurrection, which *is* the good news. But it doesn't go as far as it should in our lives. That good news has radical implications on how we live life here and now. When you say, "I believe in Jesus. He died and rose again for me," that's the gospel. But that good news should change our lives now, not just our future destinations. It should make this world a little more peaceful, a little more like paradise. It should shape us to be a little more like peacemakers.

That means we not only make peace but also don't cause drama. As a follower of Jesus, it's in no way acceptable to continue to exist as a maker or encourager of rivalry and conflict.

Conflict Makers or Peacemakers?

Following Jesus demands that we be painfully honest with ourselves: Are we conflict makers or peacemakers? (Ouch! I know, I know. That's a nasty question.) Becoming people of peace doesn't happen by accident (even though some of us might find that it comes more naturally than for others). But because becoming peacemakers is so wrapped up with the countercultural work of Christ's redemption, it takes intentional work. Sometimes the hard part is owning how far we are from it—the little things, the mundane situations in which we should have made peace but didn't.[12] Maybe we even made things *worse* through our frustration at a world that wasn't as it should be.

There are telltale signs to indicate which type of person you are. First of all, how much discord are you finding yourself involved in? How much discord are you unilaterally creating in your relationships, in your workplace?

Finding biblical ways to justify discord doesn't count. Trust me; I know firsthand, because I've tried. I know the Bible well enough to come up with things like, "I was just exercising my boldness in Christ," "I was speaking truth," and "I was refusing to live in fear." These are cop-outs. If we use them, we're afraid to look our own immaturity in the eye.

Of course, don't live in fear. *Do* use your voice. But even at his most controversial, Jesus never stirred up discord for the sake of stirring up discord or just because someone rubbed him the wrong way. He was always interested in inau-

---

[12] Like my trip to the airport.

gurating his Father's kingdom, which was a kingdom of shalom.

We see this in Isaiah's famous prophecy about Jesus, the one we hear at Christmastime every year:

> Unto us a Child is born,
> Unto us a Son is given;
> And the government will be upon His shoulder.
> And His name will be called
> Wonderful, Counselor, Mighty God,
> Everlasting Father, Prince of Peace.
> Of the increase of His government and peace
> There will be no end,
> Upon the throne of David and over His kingdom,
> To order it and establish it with judgment and justice
> From that time forward, even forever.
> The zeal of the LORD of hosts will perform this.[13]

Did you notice that Isaiah links Jesus's peacemaking with holding the government up? (Isaiah is *not* talking about our government, by the way, or any human government.) This is how we harmonize Jesus's decisive, bold, temple-table-flipping qualities with the fact that he's the Prince of Peace. With Jesus, peace is never passive. As members of the body of Christ with unique gifts and talents and passions, peacemaking requires that we all find distinct avenues within this world for being *proactive* makers of peace.

The key for each one of us is to seize our areas of influ-

---

[13] Isaiah 9:6–7.

ence and proactively make peace in those places. That's one of the reasons God made each of us unique. We have unique ways of getting at peace in the world, so that in small ways, through millions of unique followers of Jesus, the world is being transformed by Jesus through us.[14]

I realize making peace in a world like ours is a daunting task. Too often we don't get involved at all because we feel as though the task is too big and we'll never get anywhere. I love what Mother Teresa of Calcutta said: "If you can't feed a hundred people, then feed just one."

As we walk with Jesus, we have to learn how to just *be,* how to just take the step we're on, how to do what's right in front of us, how to just do the next thing—in everything. We need to reject the cultural lie that change always has to be a massive overhaul rather than incremental over time. Let us embrace, not despise, the days of small beginnings.

It is never inconsequential to see one person's life changed. When we are peacemakers, when we do good for one person and that individual extends that kindness to somebody else, before you know it, as you continue to walk in this peace-

---

[14] Even though I make it clear that God isn't asking us to judge others by how they vote, I'm a big fan of people being passionate about life, and one of those passions is politics for some people. But I'm also very concerned with the way we hold that passion as followers of Jesus. The world we live in says that if you have a political bent, you should be conflict driven, and that mindset filters into the body of Christ. So instead of being peacemakers within politics and political discussions, we contribute to the madness. For sure, we ought to have different visions than the rest of the world of how things should work. But an angry, divisive Christian in the political sphere is useless for God's kingdom work. We have to hold our political views and channel our passions in such a way that we are still making peace even when we disagree with somebody on how everything is supposed to work.

making journey that God has you on, you'll see peace grow around you like you'd never imagined.

In America during the 1950s, a group of parents and doctors were grieved by the way society treated people with serious mental disabilities. These people were put away from society, as if they were an embarrassment or would somehow infect other people. The parents and doctors hated what they saw, so they began to invite others to honor people with mental disabilities, help resource them, and teach them how to live in homes. Parent groups throughout the country met in Minneapolis and organized the National Association of Parents and Friends of Retarded Children,[15] which later became what is known today as the ARC.

God was inviting that group of parents and doctors to save these mentally disabled people from the destruction of anonymity and meaningless lives. Since then, across the world there are more than three hundred ARCs helping people with mental disabilities. Through the group's work and the contributions of others in the field, our culture has shifted its attitude toward the mentally disabled. Instead of fearing them and alienating them, now we see them as vulnerable community members we need to care for. We understand how special they are. A generation later, tens of thousands of lives are being touched. But it began with a few people being willing to take a step. They brought peace to lives filled with conflict.

On the other hand, have you seen how human attempts to make peace can go sideways and make bigger messes? That's

---

[15] I should note that *retarded* did not always have the negative or abusive connotations that it carries today.

because the only way to truly make peace is to be at peace with God first. That's the downside of the hippie movement. They've got the right idea—we *should* give peace a chance—but if we don't have peace with God, we can't have true and lasting external peace.

Of course, Jesus's atonement for the sins of the world is the ultimate act of peacemaking. But the implications of what it means to be at peace with God are determined by the choices we make each day.

A Tall Order?

If peacemaking is sounding like a taller and taller order, I totally get it—that's how it sounds to me too. I'm not saying that peacemaking is easy. But let's look at the blessing Jesus promises us! Peacemakers shall be called what? Sons of God.[16]

Peace characterizes God's family. As men and women of God, as those who are born again, as God's kids, we *should be* peacemakers. It's in our "DNA" as God's family members.

But it's the peace of *Jesus* we make and proclaim, not something we've made up. Not just a better feeling or a new mindset. It includes justice and mercy and *joy*. Think about Isaiah 52:7: "How beautiful upon the mountains are the feet of him who brings good news, who proclaims peace, who

---

[16] Because we live in a culture that is sensitive to gender distinctions, let me just say that when the Bible says "sons of God," it means sons *and* daughters of God. This was just the language of the time and is in no way exclusive of women. Women are just as much children of God as men are. I think we all know that, but I wanted to mention it in case you were wondering.

brings glad tidings of good things, who proclaims salvation, who says to Zion, 'Your God reigns!' "

Proclaiming the good news of Jesus always goes hand in hand with making peace, because in some sense, they are one and the same. I can't proclaim the good news apart from making peace, because Jesus's life, death, and resurrection secured my salvation *through* making peace between me and the Father. I can't make peace apart from proclaiming the good news, because any peace apart from the Prince of Peace is temporary.

People intuitively know this to be true, even if they explicitly deny Christ. If you look at any movement of reconciliation—whether it's racial, ethnic, or based on gender—when someone speaks of a philosophy of reconciliation, Jesus is almost always mentioned. You know why? Because he is the ultimate example of self-sacrifice. And in order for peace to be made, somebody has to be self-sacrificial. In our conflict, somebody has to be willing to take it on the proverbial chin in aspects of reconciliation.

As I write this, my country of America seems more divided than any time in recent memory. If we were going to pray (and I think we should!) that the US government and its partisan polarization of Democrats and Republicans would actually work together, like we were taught back in elementary school, both sides would need to do what?

Sacrifice. Think of something bigger than themselves. *Make peace.*

Peaceful Sacrifice

Think for a minute about sacrifice. Sacrifice is what God did to make peace with us. To heal the brokenness of the world, Jesus sacrificed his *life*. He knew we'd still get things wrong, but he died so reconciliation between God and man could be accomplished.

Every semisuccessful attempt at peace since then has mandated sacrifice. Think about how many people sacrificed deeply for racial equality in the civil rights movement. Think about how many people gave up their lives trying to protect the Jewish people during World War II.

Jesus reveals to us that peacemaking is costly, which is exactly why so many people don't do it today. You realize that if you want to be a proactive peacemaker in the brokenness in your family, at your job, in this world, you have to be willing to *die* a little for it to happen.

You can't give what you don't have. Our culture doesn't value peacemaking at all, because we don't have any models of it in our secular society. We don't have any models of it because we've divorced ourselves from the quintessential peacemaker, Jesus. That's why the world needs the body of Christ to be makers of peace.

It should come as no surprise, then, as we turn to the fruit of the Spirit, that the fruit of peacemaking is faithfulness.

In a world rife with conflict, often people *want* to make peace, but at some point they fatigue in the process. We've become instant-gratification people. If peace doesn't happen in a moment, we're like, "Forget this. It's not working."

Peacemaking requires faithfulness—determined obedience over the long haul. You and I need to realize that making peace is costly, and we have to be willing to continue to pay the cost.

Think about this in your own relationship with Jesus. How faithful has any of us been to Jesus? True, we try our best, and he delights in that. But I don't think any of us has been 100 percent rock solid every single day since the moment we said yes to Jesus for the first time.

But how faithful has Jesus been to us?

Completely faithful.

Eternally faithful.

Jesus doesn't quit when it gets hard or when he gets tired; he just keeps on showing up.

That's how peacemaking happens. You have to be willing to just keep on showing up, good times and bad times, when you feel like it, when you don't.

Proverbs 28:20 says, "A faithful man will abound with blessings." Pretty cool, right? Yet faithfulness is in short supply in our generation because faithfulness, like peacemaking, is hard. Faithfulness *costs*. That's what makes it so important.

Being married to the same person through every up and down of life is a big cost, isn't it? Being a faithful friend has a cost to it. I've heard it said that you'll know who your friends are by who's around when everything goes wrong. It's easy to be a great friend when everything's awesome, but when things are hitting the skids? That's when you really know who your friends are.

That is faithfulness—the ability to continue, to abide, to show up and be there and *stay* there even when things get bad. Especially when they get bad!

My friends, Jesus is the most faithful person who's ever lived. I mean, when followers of Jesus make terrible decisions, does Jesus ever just abandon them? No. When Peter denied Jesus, Jesus *restored* him and cooked him a meal! David dishonored God, but God wasn't done with him or his family. Heck, at the end of the day, Jesus was born through his lineage!

Here's the thing. Obviously, Jesus is perfect and we are not. But God invites each of us, although we are imperfect, to just keep showing up. When I think of "showing up," I always envision Bill Ritchie, the founding pastor of the church I lead, Crossroads. He showed up to preach for forty years, Sunday after Sunday (and Sunday nights and Wednesday nights), in times of great blessing and in times of great challenge. His wife, Betty, *still* volunteers in our kids' ministry more than forty years later. Talk about faithfulness!

We can have these kinds of stories for our lives, too, but we have to stick it out when life gets hard. I feel as though faithfulness is one of the lost arts in society today. But Jesus is so faithful. And because he has always been faithful to us, he invites us to keep showing up—to keep fighting for what we know is right.

Our culture says, "If it's too much trouble, throw it out and buy a new one."

You know what? Our culture is wrong. (Gasp!)

Many of us know what it's like to be treated that way—as if we're disposable. We're there as long as someone needs us, and then we're just discarded and the person finds a new toy, a cleaner toy, a toy that doesn't have history. But God has called us to a beautifully different way.

Same with the crazy happy fight to make peace in your

marriage. You fight for your kids. You fight for your coworkers. You fight for the relationships that God has given you. It doesn't mean that you show up and it's always perfect. *You're* definitely not perfect, and neither am I. You don't handle it right every time, but you keep showing up. That's what faithfulness is. And if you show up long enough with a humble heart and keep on going, you'll get somewhere.

When I look at the world in which we live today, my friends, my hope and prayer is that the people of God will rise up and make peace—that we would be drivers of universal flourishing and wholeness in the kingdom that God is bringing to bear in our present reality.

When people think of followers of Jesus, what if they would say to themselves, *They're just like Jesus who makes peace*? What if we showed up day after day, week after week, month after month, year after year, decade after decade, generation after generation, with the good news and what that good news implies?

That sounds like a beautiful life to me.

9

The Crazy Happy Way of Gentleness

Blessed are those who are persecuted for righteousness' sake,
For theirs is the kingdom of heaven.

—Matthew 5:10

The fruit of the spirit is . . . gentleness.

—Galatians 5:22–23

I love music. Always have, always will. That's why I talk about it every chance I get.

Before I was called into the ministry, my career path—my entire life's pursuit—was to play music. In middle school, all I ever wanted to do was be a rock star. I grew up in the MTV generation, and nothing was cooler to me than the guitarists I saw shredding in the music videos. Not to mention, guitar players got all the girls.

I quickly discovered that playing guitar was extremely complicated, though, with all those little strings, so I settled on drums. But that was pretty short lived. It only lasted until my parents decided they couldn't take my practicing any-more. So maybe a week or two? And that's how I ended up a bass player. It had just four strings, which I thought would be easier to master.[1] Every band needed a bass player, so there were opportunities to jam. And I could practice it without turning it up to eleven and getting yelled at because of all the noise I created.

Virtually right out of the gate, I started playing for bands. As I said before, bass players were in demand! I played bass for multiple bands, and by the time I was a senior in high school, the bands I played in were really popular.[2] For a while, hundreds of young people were turning up for our shows, and we played a lot of shows. So that equals a lot of money for a high school senior!

The shows, the girls, the glory of it all—it went to my head pretty quickly. So it didn't take me very long to decide I wanted to make a living as a professional musician. I mean, it's *really* fun, everybody loves you, you're the center of at-tention, and you make a lot of money. That's how I saw it at the time, so it felt like a dream come true.

The only thing was, I wasn't that good. I knew some songs and could make it through a gig,[3] but I knew I had to get *good* at bass to make it big. It's one thing to be up onstage with a massive amplifier and bang your head while all your

[1]   News flash, mastering any instrument is very hard.

[2]   The only thing I didn't realize was the reason they were popular: that everyone in high school just wanted something to do and there wasn't a lot to do. But what we didn't know didn't hurt us.

[3]   Plus, at that time I had my first head of dreads, which looked solid.

friends scream like you're the coolest thing. It's a whole other thing entirely to play music with sensitivity and artistry for people who buy tickets.

So I got serious. I started taking lessons. I bought the upright bass that I mentioned in chapter 5. I got into jazz, and then there was a slew of consequences I never could have predicted. For instance, when I was in high school, I'd play a thirty-minute set at some all-ages dive venue, and I'd make about five hundred bucks. And then I learned how to actually play my instrument, started playing jazz . . . and I'd make fifty bucks in three hours. You realize what a mess that is from a career perspective, right?

When I met my wife, I had a double-whammy career when it comes to making money: I was church planting *and* playing music on the side. At the time, Lynn's uncle John (a seriously no-nonsense guy, who I respect) said, "So, how are you going to provide for my niece?" And you know me. I said, "Oh, God's going to provide." Unfazed, Uncle John fired back, "Well, that might be true, but how are *you* gonna provide? I heard you're a musician and a pastor. None of that's gonna pay the bills."

Reality Checks

Uncle John wasn't very far off from the truth. It's just funny to me now, because if I had kept on playing the music I was playing in high school, who knows? Maybe I'd be a multimillionaire by now! Instead, I learned to play my instrument really well and became your classic starving jazz musician. When you pursue something with high expectations and something entirely different happens, it's a sobering reality check.

The good news for followers of Jesus is, if you're living up to the highest ideals of what God has called you to, you don't need to worry about where life lands you. You can rest assured that God is reworking all your circumstances to his own good purposes.

Living beautifully in Jesus means we can have hope no matter what goes on in life. No matter where we thought we'd end up, we are in exactly the place we're supposed to be when we walk with Jesus.

We've seen again and again that the way of Jesus is the most beautiful way we can live. We also keep running into the fact that what God sees as beautiful and what our culture sees as beautiful are not the same. Unfortunately, what God sees as beautiful is sometimes so off-putting to our society that people will not only disagree but also actively fight against it.

This chapter is one of *those*. So without further ado, let's talk about persecution! (Cue peppy game-show music!)

By the time we get here to Matthew 5:10, Jesus has given us seven surprising ways to live crazy happy. And so far, even the more challenging of his ideas about mourning and meekness haven't been *too* hard to swallow. But being persecuted for righteousness?

C'mon, Jesus.

You could say it this way: if we're persecuted for anything, you and I should be persecuted for the right things.[4] No one

---

4   Sound familiar? This is not much different from what we discussed in chapter 5—that you and I need to hunger and thirst for the right things. We will pursue what we long for, so if we long for the right things, we'll pursue them and walk in them. So Jesus is saying, "If you get persecuted, let it be about me and walking righteously, not because you did something wrong."

wants to be persecuted, but if it happens, shouldn't it happen for righteousness?

Persecution is when somebody actively seeks to thwart what we're doing. Now, when I say we should be persecuted for the *right* things, it's because, unfortunately, many times when people talk about being persecuted, they're not being persecuted for righteousness' sake; they're being persecuted for other things. Like maybe because they're being a jerk. And there's a big difference. I hear all the time, "Well, I got let go from my job because I'm a Christian."

I'm like, "Okay, so what happened?" And they'll say, "Well, you know, I'm supposed to be working there, and I was telling my coworkers about Jesus, and I got fired." And usually I say, "Well, they don't hire you to tell them about Jesus; they hire you to do a job. How'd you do at your job?" And the answer is a mumbled, "Okay, I guess."

If you do your job well and you tell people about Jesus along the way, your employer most likely won't get mad. But if you don't do your job or you do it poorly, you will get fired. It's not for righteousness' sake; it's because you're not doing your job! Even at a church, if an employee was only ever talking about Jesus and not doing the actual job he or she was hired to do, that wouldn't fly. Let's not be that kind of person.

If you're a Christian, you should never be a jerk, plain and simple. But here's the thing: if you're a Christian and not a jerk, sometimes people still won't like you. And, my friends, that's not really all that fun, is it? Sometimes choosing to walk in obedience to God by living righteously is all it takes to experience persecution from other people.

We already looked at righteousness in chapter 5. If you'll

recall, righteousness refers to anything that is *right*. It is proper conduct before God. It's even more than just being good. Righteousness is an entire orientation of life that is toward God and toward his will. That's no small order, considering that the pressure of conformity in our culture is so strong and relentless.

The heart of righteousness is that no matter what anyone else says we're supposed to do, if Jesus says he actually wants us to live differently, that's what we do. The reason our modern American Christianity is not biblical Christianity is because we've allowed ourselves to conform to principles that aren't biblical. We've strayed from the simple reality of what it means to follow Jesus.[5]

We've all found ourselves cutting a few corners on the way Jesus calls us to live in order to keep the status quo of what's going on culturally. Sadly, this isn't even persecution; it's just us caving in to the pressure to conform. Conformity always leads to mediocrity.[6] Meanwhile, across the globe, people face arrest or even death for their faith in Jesus. Now, *that's* persecution.

When I was serving in the southern part of India a number of years ago, I met several pastors who had burn marks

---

[5] When I say American Christianity, I know I'm painting with a broad brush. There are a *ton* of great churches in America and a *ton* of amazing Christians who follow Jesus and read the Word and apply it to their lives. What I'm talking about is that, in general, the church in America is struggling with her responsibility before God to read and know his Word, take him at his word, and live it out, regardless of societal pressures that say it's dumb or irrelevant or evil or even worse.

[6] In Revelation 3:16, Jesus tells the church of Laodicea that God would spit them out of his mouth because they were apathetic and mediocre.

and scars, results of a mass persecution against the Indian church about ten years previously. And you know what they said to me? They asked me to pray for boldness for them so they could endure persecution. Think about what they didn't ask for. They didn't ask for revenge. They didn't ask for safety for their families. They didn't even ask for an end to persecution. They just wanted to see the gospel of Jesus thrive in that region, and they wanted courage to keep preaching even though they knew they would be physically harmed for doing so.

When I was in the Middle East a few years back, going to church meant pulling up to an unmarked building enclosed by barbed wire.[7] We walked through the door, and inside, five hundred believers were worshipping in three different languages, none of which was English, while armed guards stood watch outside. It was mind blowing.

In the Western world, we're blessed to practice our faith so openly. At Crossroads, the service not only happens multiple times in the physical building, but it also beams all over the world on the internet, on the TV, on the radio, on social media, and the biggest pushback we have to worry about is maybe an occasional protester or a snarky comment on Facebook.[8]

We must never forget we follow Jesus, a person who was persecuted for righteousness' sake. Our salvation comes

---

[7]   I have to be honest; it was a little freaky. But it was also kinda cool to experience.

[8]   Those comments are usually either about my great hair or my bad jokes.

from Jesus's beautiful life, lived entirely in orientation to God: "I always do those things that please my Father."[9] And they killed him for it. In the same way, as we live completely oriented to God, at certain points we will *necessarily* run in absolute conflict with the culture in which we live.

It's hard to picture what it would be like to follow Jesus at the potential cost of our lives. But you know what's funny?[10] Following Jesus is *supposed* to cost us our lives. Maybe not physically, but Jesus asks us to give up our self-styled lives and take on his crucified and resurrected life, in which we die to ourselves and live in him.

Many of us have kept our self-styled lives and tried to sprinkle a little Jesus on top. And as a result, we never run into conflict with the world in which we live—which is a big problem.

But then what do we do with Jesus when he says, "Oh how happy, oh how fortunate, oh how *blessed* are those who have been actively and aggressively persecuted for their orientation to God"? Where does that perspective fit? It doesn't.

> Jesus asks us to give up our self-styled lives and take on his crucified and resurrected life.

---

[9] See John 8:29.

[10] I mean funny in a darkly ironic sort of way.

We love to talk about how good Jesus is.[11] But Jesus is not safe sometimes. He can be dangerous. He is ferocious. And he is never driven by our culture.

A Life Too Safe

I believe that through this message, Jesus is saying to us, "Brother, sister, the way you're living is too *safe.*" The choices we make (trying to make sure everything works out for us) sometimes pit our lives against faithfulness to his gospel.

Following Jesus requires us to ask ourselves, *How am I cutting corners in my life? Am I trying to dodge the struggles that come from living for God in a world that doesn't?*

The apostle Peter knew about both conforming and being persecuted, didn't he? After all, he folded like a towel when Jesus was arrested. He straight-up denied him! But then he became a firebrand of the church, thrown in jail and even martyred for his faith. What an example of growing out of compromise! He writes in 1 Peter 3:13, "Who will harm you if you become followers of what is good?"

Makes sense—if you do what is good, no harm should come to you. Sure, that's logical. But then he says this:

> Even if you should suffer for righteousness' sake, you are blessed. "And do not be afraid of their threats, nor be troubled." But sanctify the Lord God in your hearts, and always be ready to give a defense to everyone who asks you a reason for the hope that is in you, with meekness and fear; hav-

---

[11] And don't get me wrong; he *is.* In fact, he's better than we can imagine.

ing a good conscience, that when they defame you
as evildoers, those who revile your good conduct
in Christ may be ashamed. For it is better, if it is
the will of God, to suffer for doing good than for
doing evil. (verses 14–17)

Peter was saying that if you walk righteously, no harm
should come to you. But if harm *does* come to you, at least
let it be because you know you're living the right way and not
because you're living the wrong way. How realistic is that!

We need to embrace the reality that really being a Christian will sometimes put us in conflict with the world in which
we live. Our job is not to diminish our witness in order to
conform better to that world. Instead, we must realize that,
like Jesus, we are *blessed* when the world in which we live
doesn't accept the faith that we hold. Even when, sometimes,
they flat out don't like it. Or us.

Let's revisit the flow of the Beatitudes for a second—these
simple movements to lead into the next movement, just like
the movements of a symphony. There is a logic and flow to
them. The beautiful life begins with spiritual bankruptcy,
which leaves our hearts soft enough to break for the world,
which produces meekness. In meekness, when we get to the
end of ourselves, we develop a hunger and thirst for righteousness. And Jesus promises we'll be satisfied. Because
we've been satisfied by God, we become people of mercy,
knowing we have received mercy. As God purifies our hearts,
we become peacemakers in the world—which is great until
we run into people who don't want to be at peace with us.
That gets us persecuted for righteousness' sake.

Kind of sobering, isn't it?

Can we be real for a minute? In a culture driven by comfort, this is a huge hurdle for Christians. We've been raised by a society in which people don't do the things that make them uncomfortable. Ever.[12] The things that stand in the way of you getting your way—you push those out of the way as much as you possibly can.

But when you consider our brothers and sisters in Christ all over the world who are being persecuted *right now* for their faith in Jesus, it makes all the petty things we complain about look a little small, doesn't it?

Look at the early church and the suffering endured by the world's first Christians. Back then, theologians believed that "the blood of the martyrs is the seed of the church."[13] The fire in the belly of the church was rekindled by the persecution they endured and the sacrifices they made.

Persecution purifies the church. When it costs you something, it changes the way you live. It changes your prayers. It changes the way you see God.

That's not to say we don't experience suffering today in America. We do, and it's not fair to anyone to compare pain. I'm not naive enough to glamorize persecution. I've never experienced it in a life-or-death way. Nor is it healthy to be ashamed of the blessings we enjoy here on earth, because every blessing is a gift from God and should be celebrated. But let's practice gratitude and not take it for granted either. We get a little lazy when things come too easily.

---

[12] Well, unless you count working out. But usually there are ulterior motives for that.

[13] Tertullian, *Apologeticus,* chapter 50.

Plus, in 2 Timothy 3:12, Paul wrote, "All who desire to live godly in Christ Jesus will suffer persecution." That *will* is a rough word, isn't it? Persecution *will* happen. So here's the real question for you and me: Will we follow Jesus even if people get upset with us?

Jesus's promise to his persecuted followers is interesting too: "Blessed are those who are persecuted for righteousness' sake, for theirs is the kingdom of heaven."[14]

The idea of the kingdom of heaven or the kingdom of God is the place where God reigns. Not everybody is interested in that, especially in a day and age where the overarching kingdom is the kingdom of self. This *reward* actually flies in the face of our cultural narcissism and sense of entitlement. We want it here and now, and we want the reward we think we deserve.

For God's kingdom to move in, our kingdom needs to move on.

Here's the truth, and what I really think Jesus is getting at: there can be only one kingdom reigning in your heart at any given time. So when Jesus in that classic model prayer says, "Lord, may your kingdom come and your will be done on earth as it is in heaven,"[15] he's not just asking for God's kingdom to come; he's also saying our own kingdom has to leave.

For God's kingdom to move in, our kingdom needs to

---

[14] Matthew 5:10.

[15] See Matthew 6:10.

move on. Two kingdoms trying to occupy the same space can only ever end in conflict. And if you're sitting on the throne of your life, then Jesus definitely is not.

That's always a hard one for us. Who is truly sitting on the throne of our lives? We all have to allow Jesus to take a central place in our lives. So as God's people, if we're inviting God's kingdom to reign in our hearts, *that* is the kingdom that is totally unacceptable to many people. And that's why persecution happens.

Throughout history, you can see countless examples of times when people sought to forcibly remove the kingdom of God from the world. First Christians were persecuted by the Jewish people who didn't believe that Jesus was the Messiah. Then they were persecuted by Rome.

And, of course, when Christianity became the religion of the Roman Empire in the early fourth century, the church experienced a period of relative peace. But then a group of people began to pull away from the state-sponsored church because of its corruption, and they began to live in the wilderness (they called them the Desert Fathers and Mothers). And guess what? Those people were persecuted. Likewise, the Christian church in China has faced persecution for hundreds of years.[16]

Jesus told us that Christians would be persecuted. Read his words in John 15:17–21:

> These things I command you, that you love one another.

---

[16] What's amazing, though, is that the church is flourishing in China, even under harsh persecution.

If the world hates you, you know that it hated Me before it hated you. If you were of the world, the world would love its own. Yet because you are not of the world, but I chose you out of the world, therefore the world hates you. Remember the word that I said to you, "A servant is not greater than his master." If they persecuted Me, they will also persecute you. If they kept My word, they will keep yours also. But all these things they will do to you for My name's sake, because they do not know Him who sent me.

See, this is why our culture needs to hear the teachings of Jesus. He's totally real about the paradoxes of life. He's essentially saying, "Love one another. But even if you love one another, people are going to hate you."

Our job is to simply respond to Jesus—to live only how he wants us to live. We have to accept that others will feel how they feel about that. Our challenge is not to try to make everybody happy; it's to live with love and faithfulness.

The beautiful life in Christ is all about us seeking *God's* pleasure in how we live and looking out for ways that he can be praised and glorified by the choices we make. If Jesus isn't the end-all and be-all authority over our lives, then we're trying to let everything else in the world around us drive our relationship with God. It never works.

Our challenge is not to try to make everybody happy; it's to live with love and faithfulness.

I think many of us have lost that art of living for God's approval rather than humanity's. We live as if we're on a talent show, like *American Idol: Life Edition,* waiting for someone else to vote on how we live. We lose all sense of identity.

We're so busy trying to make everyone happy, trying to make the kids happy, trying to make the parents happy, trying to make the boss happy.[17] But that insecurity is the total opposite of what life in Christ is supposed to be.

So can we be honest? Can we own the fact that our culturally acceptable pop Christianity is disturbing when we compare it to what Jesus calls a blessed life? We're not willing to be the blessed ones who are persecuted for righteousness' sake, because we're trying so hard to accommodate another kingdom, where the kingdom of God is unacceptable.

So the harsh reality is, if we find our lives lining up with the kingdom of the world, we're not part of the kingdom of God. That's what I hate about this chapter: I have to lay that out there. We aren't called to be our culture's vision of what we ought to be. Our job is to be in the world and to be salt and light in the midst of it.

Now, you will *love* this.

How should we respond to this persecution we'll undoubtedly face?

---

[17] I believe that too many pastors spend their whole lives trying to make their congregations happy, and they wonder why the church is dying.

Dun dun dun!

The fruit of persecution for righteousness is . . .

Gentleness.

Underwhelmed? Hoping for fire from heaven? Nope. We respond to persecution with gentleness!

This is why I love Jesus, why I love being a Christian, because it's so crazy by anyone else's logic.[18] The world responds to things proportionally. So, in effect, if you slap me, I slap you back, because it's only fair. And we don't always stop there, with proportionality. It gets worse. Often we see relationships ruled by the law of escalation: not only do we want to get even, we want to one-up each other.

And what is Jesus's response? *Be gentle.* I mean, this is back to the "crazy" part of crazy happy, right?

Interestingly, gentleness means basically the same thing as meekness, which we defined in chapter 4 as "strength under control." Gentleness is the ability to embrace people where they are without being aggressive toward them. So in the context of what Jesus is saying about persecution, gentleness is our willingness to submit ourselves to God and also bless others, even if they're aggressive toward you.

This is good news for all of us because, let's be real, every one of us is fragile. Even the toughest of us is more fragile than we'd like people to believe.

Demonstrated Gentleness

Demonstrating gentleness toward others, especially when they're against us, means we're walking in the humility

---

[18] I often joke that I have the spiritual gift of mischief. I am in it for the shenanigans.

needed to handle others with care in the ways we speak and the ways we act. Gentleness is a determination to encourage and bless others as we interact with them. So in the face of persecution, we shouldn't be angry, meeting aggression with aggression. When we meet aggression with aggression, we only create more aggression. But when we meet aggression with gentleness, we stop escalation in its tracks.[19]

In some ways, this was the brilliance of Martin Luther King Jr.'s philosophy during the civil rights movement. He knew that to heal his country and address systemic oppression, he had to stop the cycle of aggression and retaliation—not by passively accepting the status quo, and not by violently fighting against it, but by living for the kingdom of God here on earth, in gentleness, meekness, and peacefulness.

When we choose to live beautifully, we break the most grotesque cycles of injustice we see in our world. Dr. King learned this truth from his Savior, Jesus.

Jesus is textbook gentleness. The Bible says that when he was arrested, "as a sheep to the slaughter . . . He opened not His mouth."[20] If there were ever a person in the history of humanity who could have laid out everything each of his persecutors ever did and held it over their heads, it was Jesus of Nazareth. But he chose not to defend himself. Why? Because he wasn't looking for anyone's validation, except his heavenly Father's.

And, brothers and sisters, even if we never contend with

---

[19] It's hard to have a one-sided argument, isn't it?

[20] Acts 8:32.

persecution, the goal is the same: God is still calling us all to be gentle.

So as followers of Jesus in this world, we need to show ourselves as gentle with our politics, gentle with our spouses, gentle with our kids, gentle with our grandkids, gentle with our neighbors, gentle at our places of work and worship, gentle wherever we go.

In 1 Thessalonians 2:7–8, Paul said, "We were gentle among you, just as a nursing mother cherishes her own children. So, affectionately longing for you, we were well pleased to impart to you not only the gospel of God, but also our own lives, *because you had become dear to us.*"

Paul was gentle to this church because the people had become dear to him. Our job, as followers of Jesus in a dying world, is to let this world become dear to us, that we might demonstrate Christ's own gentleness to everyone we meet. This world is dear to Jesus—so dear that he took all the sins of humanity upon himself on the cross.[21] And what's amazing is that if, God forbid, we do encounter persecution, he would want our persecutors to become dear to us, that we might respond in gentleness.

Jesus died not just for the persecution we experience at the hands of others but for our persecution of others, too, in our own rebellion. And now he's inviting us to let his Spirit of gentleness breathe through our lives to a hurting, fragile world.

And let's not miss the fact that usually aggression is a

---

[21] And that absolutely includes the issues of our present cultural moment.

symptom of deeper hurt or fear. Aggression reveals a person's fragility. And when you respond to someone who is hurt and scared in an aggressive way, he or she gets more scared and more aggressive.

Jesus is the great de-escalator, and he's calling you and me to that more excellent way.

The best thing about the crazy happy life? Jesus never says, "You got that? Good luck!" Every day he walks with us and empowers us by his Spirit, showing us the way and helping birth his gentleness in the face of our persecution.

Jesus himself lived this out as he gently prayed for forgiveness for those who crucified him. "Forgive them, Father, for they know not what they do."

As we follow Jesus and are transformed, this same gentleness adorns our life. The crazy happy life is one in which we respond to persecution with gentleness. And when that happens, the crazy happy life of Jesus is on display for all who have eyes to see.

10

The Crazy Happy Way of Self-Control

Blessed are you when they revile and persecute you, and say all kinds of evil against you falsely for My sake. Rejoice and be exceedingly glad, for great is your reward in heaven, for so they persecuted the prophets who were before you.
—Matthew 5:11–12

The fruit of the Spirit is . . . self-control.
—Galatians 5:22–23

Everything in life involves some risk.

When I was a senior in high school, I was nominated for homecoming king.[1] As part of the process, each nominee had to have a "Get to know me" video. I had an early advantage because I had been taking TV production as an elective.

---

[1] The sheer absurdity of that statement still makes me chuckle. I actually wore plaid pants and a gas-station-attendant shirt to the homecoming dance.

And, trust me, I planned on taking full advantage of my video-editing skills.

As people's videos started to roll in, I realized that all the other videos were essentially the same. Their favorite song was in the background.[2] They were telling you about themselves. Honestly, it strikes me now as the equivalent of a video someone might post to a dating site today. You know: "My name is Brian. I like to work out. I am a very accomplished athlete. My parents bought me a cool car. And I think my . . . [*flex*] . . . biceps are my best feature."[3]

So I settled on a plan. It began with a still photo: me with a big goofy smile. "My name is Daniel Fusco, and I'm a really friendly guy." Then the way-too-loud-and-obnoxious punk music began. For the next eighty seconds, the entire video had quick edits of me kissing people.[4] It was epic.

But as we were filming, I knew that to truly make this video unforgettable, I needed to get a video of me kissing Mr. Lundquist. Why? Because he was well known as one of the sternest and snarkiest teachers in my high school. Weighing in at a solid 260 pounds, Mr. Lundquist used his history classroom to humble us as though he were a military drill sergeant carrying a high school textbook. Between his quick wit and biting sarcasm, it was not uncommon for him to literally bring students to tears. Then he would laugh a huge

---

[2] It was the early '90s in New Jersey, so lots of dance music and hard rock.

[3] For the record, I just made all that up. But that was a pretty honest take on the videos.

[4] It was also the apex of my movie career. It should be noted that all the kisses were on the cheek, for those of you concerned about my holiness.

belly laugh and say, "Oh, come on. I'm just messing with you."[5]

So I just *had* to have Mr. Lundquist in my video. I figured that the best way to accomplish this was to tell him my plan and make a joke about it. One day he opened the door and said, rolling his eyes, "Hey, Fusco, I heard a rumor that they are taking videos of you kissing people." I seized my moment and said, "Funny you should say that, Mr. Lundquist. I was thinking I need to get you in my video." His face turned red. "If you even try, I will get you suspended, and I will fail you in my class. Say goodbye to college, Fusco."

Well, that escalated quickly, right? I was bummed but not surprised. Mr. Lundquist was true to form.

But hey, everything involves risk. Nothing ventured, nothing gained. And no one ever became immortal without going for broke.

So I got myself mentally prepared and sufficiently hyped up. I had my buddy Fred set up a bit down the hall with the camera. I figured that as Mr. Lundquist walked down the hall toward Fred, I would come up around him all ninja-like and plant a wet one on his gray-and-black beard. Sure enough, the time was right, so I made my move.

It all happened in slow motion. I leaned in, but Mr. Lundquist was wicked fast. He leaned away. I missed by about an inch. *Rats!* He just leered at me, which made me very nervous. And then he chuckled and just walked away.[6]

---

[5] Mr. Lundquist was the kind of teacher who would actually encourage you to get into a hallway fight so he could break it up and inflict a little pain.

[6] To be honest, his lack of comment was quite intimidating.

So Fred and I went back to the TV production lab. I felt as though I'd just lost the Super Bowl. I was dejected and a little bit unnerved. As we watched the footage of all the kisses, I must have rewatched "The Attempt" fifty times. So close, but so far.

But then it dawned on me that I actually had something *better*.

As my video was drawing to a close, I decided to have it crescendo with three stunning still shots of kisses. The final shot was the most outrageous. It was me trying to kiss Lundquist: me all puckered up, and him pulling his face away cringing. Because he explicitly didn't want to be in my video, I put a big red rectangle over his eyes with the word *Censored* in bold within the rectangle. It was perfect.

We had a special assembly to present the videos to the school. When it was my turn, my video was unlike anyone else's, obviously. But I was just waiting for that last frame. What would happen when he, let alone the rest of the school, saw this?

My eyes were glued to Mr. Lundquist when that final still shot appeared on the projection screen. His eyes got really big. Everyone roared with laughter. Everyone knew that it was Lundquist. Then the teachers who were standing near him started to laugh so hard that tears were rolling down their cheeks. Lundquist then started to laugh hysterically. He looked over at me with a big smile and mouthed, "Great job!"

Funnily enough, from that day forward, Mr. Lundquist and I got along famously. And as it turned out, I was voted homecoming king. I guess being a really friendly guy has its benefits!

Good Risks

Every real decision has an element of risk. Every real decision has consequences. And the higher the stakes of the decisions we're making, the more significant the consequences can be. No matter how hard we try to reduce our uncertainty or how calculated we are, we can't ever guarantee the consequences of our decisions. So we ultimately have to weigh our values and desires against the potential consequences (and the effort involved) and pick whatever is more important.

Everything in life comes down to counting the costs of our decisions and looking ahead to where things will land us when they ultimately blossom and come to fruition.

Some of us (me included) often make decisions first with our gut or our emotions or by what feels important in the moment without anticipating the potential consequences. And that's what makes life hard as it relates to the decisions we make. We don't always think through the potential risks as much as we should. Everything in life comes down to counting the costs of our decisions and looking ahead to where things will land us when they ultimately blossom and come to fruition.

A good friend of mine recently went home to be with the Lord. He died because of a series of lung ailments. The problems started when he was a child, but as he got older, he made decisions along the way that exacerbated his preexisting condition. He was cautioned to take care of his lungs. But he smoked regularly, and as his lung condition worsened, he was told by a doctor that if he didn't give up smoking, he would die.

I remember he stopped smoking for about five hours after that conversation . . . and then picked it right back up again. When I found out he was smoking again, I couldn't believe it. I got on his case, because I loved the guy! I reminded him of what the doctor had told him, but he just turned to me and said, "Bro, I really don't know that I care that much."

That probably sounds unbelievable to many of us. And I can share with you that, yes, it was heartbreaking for me to hear. I was floored. But that's not the only one of those stories I have. Those kinds of situations are not even uncommon for a pastor, to tell you the truth. Many of us are making all kinds of decisions that have huge consequences, and we're not really counting the cost of what those decisions will mean down the line. Maybe it's health related like it was for my friend, or maybe it's in relationships or financial choices, but we all make decisions and many times don't count the costs as we should.

Even following Jesus has risks. But then, *not* following Jesus has risks too.

Some people teach that if you follow Jesus, everything you want in life will fall into place. Not only does that do damage to the name of Jesus (because it's not really how it works and it's not biblical), but in a material culture like ours, that idea is way too appealing. However, there's a grain of truth in that kind of teaching, and it's this: if you follow Jesus, everything *will* be perfect—perfectly the way God wants it to be, that is.

One thing that's challenging about Jesus is he isn't the God of affirmation of everything we think. He won't always agree with whatever we want. But he *is* the God of transformation. He takes our desires and meets us there, but he loves us too much to leave us that way.

So, ultimately, if you *do* follow Jesus, your life *is* perfect in the sense that what God wants for your life actually comes to pass. But at least some of it—and as time goes on in this adventure with Jesus, I think a lot of it—isn't what we would've chosen if left up to our own devices.

As we come to our last pairing—Beatitudes with the fruit of the Spirit—on this incredible journey toward the life God calls beautiful, we see that Jesus laid out the risk that comes from following him.

In the previous chapter, we caught a glimpse of this. Jesus has already told us at this point that we may face persecution for righteousness' sake. What Jesus does with this ninth beatitude is take the abstract, the potential of persecution we talked about, and make it concrete. He also moves from speaking about persecution in the third person, "Blessed are those who are persecuted," to second person, "Blessed are you when persecution happens to you."

Jesus wants to move us past the theoretical to the practical. He drives his truth home and leaves it at the doorstep of our lives so we have no choice but to respond to it.

I know, you're saying, *Ugh, Fusco, I was willing to hang in there with you for one chapter of persecution stuff, but another one? Are you crazy?*

Stay with me. Most of life is lived at the crossroads, when we reach any kind of a life decision and it forces us to choose whether or not we'll follow Jesus. Let me say that again: *most of life is lived at the crossroads of whether or not we will follow Jesus!*

So in this ninth and final beatitude, Jesus gets not only concrete but also personal. "Blessed are *you* when they revile and persecute you. . . . Rejoice and be exceedingly glad, for great is *your* reward in heaven."

We saw earlier that our response to persecution ought to be gentleness, and now Jesus is taking it even a step further: be joyful when you're challenged.

And, actually, Jesus isn't talking about persecution here in just a physical sense. He adds to it. There's reviling and evil speaking going on. We're talking about criticism. We're talking about insults. We're talking about slander. We're talking about deeply hurtful trash talking.

Yet Jesus says, "Be joyful."

In God's eyes, a beautiful life is one that does not respond to evil speaking with even more evil speaking. It's not a life that when you are insulted, you flay the other person in return. No, a life that's beautiful to God is the kind of life that when you're slandered, you take it on the chin. And even more than that, you are joyful.

Now, am I the only person who thinks that's kind of out there? I mean, it's one thing to be spoken ill of and take it like a pro. It's another thing to *rejoice* in the midst of it. But that's what the beautiful life is really all about.

As we talked about before, it's important to start by searching our own hearts to see if there is anything in our actions that might provoke anger from people. But if our conscience is clear and we're persecuted only for being in step with Jesus, then we've got reason to rejoice.

When we follow Jesus, we are making a choice. One of the risks of following Jesus is that not everyone is going to like the *way* you follow him. And not everyone is going to understand what God is doing in your life or what he has called you to. I've experienced that with some of my friends and family, and I'm sure you have as well. And guess what? When has anybody ever understood all that God is doing in anyone's life? In the process, we learn in real time right where we live and move—not only to endure the conflict but also to find joy in the midst of it.

See, joy is not everything working out the way you want it to; joy is what happens when you know that your God is good, even when everyone else is evil, like the reviling and persecuting Jesus was talking about. And you realize God's got something that he's doing in you, in the midst of the stuff you're going through.

We live in a world where we get challenged for all sorts of things we do. But for some reason today, the people of God tend to slink away from those getting upset with them for their faith. We might stand up to the neighborhood association if they don't like our paint color. And nobody thinks twice about people arguing about politics. But the moment someone disagrees with our faith in Jesus, we're like, "Oh, I probably shouldn't talk about Jesus anymore." And that, my friends, is something God wants to help us get over. Because Jesus said, "Oh how happy, oh how fortunate are you when they revile you, when they speak evil falsely of you for my name's sake, when they persecute you."

This same idea comes up in James 1:2–5: "Consider it

pure joy, my brothers and sisters, whenever you face trials of many kinds, because you know that the testing of your faith produces perseverance. Let perseverance finish its work so that you may be mature and complete, not lacking anything. If any of you lacks wisdom, you should ask God, who gives generously to all without finding fault, and it will be given to you" (NIV).

James says, "Listen, when you fall into trials, when reviling and slandering and all this stuff happens to you, when you're persecuted, count it all as joy." Why? All of it has a purpose. The testing of your faith will produce patience and perseverance in your life. Patience and perseverance will mature you so that you're not lacking anything. And then James pivots a little bit and reminds us that if we do find ourselves lacking in some way, we can ask for wisdom because God will give it.

So if we are never seeing those tests and trials, if the reviling and persecuting never happen, we can thank God, but we also need to question if we're living for Jesus the way he's asking us to.

In God's economy, problems are not just problems. He leverages problems and makes them purposeful. He wants to grow us up! I'm not trying to say it's easy. We don't have to *like* what we're experiencing in life all the time; we just have to trust that God has a plan. That's joy.[7]

If you're anything like me, I think we're all secretly hoping that our spiritual growth will occur the way phone software

---

[7]   As a side note—and this is hard to believe—but sometimes God is actually answering our prayers through the struggles we're experiencing. We just don't see the end product yet. That's why trust is such a big thing with God.

updates do these days: automatically, in our sleep. Wouldn't that be amazing? We'd just wake up and—boom!—we're spiritually mature.

But the spiritual life doesn't work that way, does it?

When we put our faith and trust in Jesus, we are perfected by his finished work and cleansed from all unrighteousness. But the implementation of Christ's life in us happens every single day, in all the most seemingly mundane moments, as well as the difficult ones.

Sometimes we forget that you and I follow a persecuted Messiah. We follow a man who, on every single page of the Gospels, was challenged and pushed against. There were many more people who didn't receive him or believe in him than people who embraced him. But for the joy that was set before him, he kept going.

When we considered saying yes to Jesus, usually all we heard was, "Jesus is here for you—your needs, your failures, your shortcomings. Jesus has forgiven you and loves you and will carry you." Basically, we hear, "It's all about you." But after we walk with Jesus and start to be transformed into his image, the more we go down the road called sanctification, we start to realize that it's not about us at all. It's about his heart for us, sure. But at the core, it's about everyone else *but* us.

His suffering has become our suffering. When you and I are reviled and slandered and persecuted, we need to remember that we're partaking in Christ's sufferings.

But we don't walk alone when we suffer. Jesus is quick to remind us of the suffering endured by saints who have gone before us. See, part of living a beautiful life is stepping into the eternal, organic reality of the redeemed people of God.

And when you remember that you're not the only one, your whole perspective changes.

We live in a self-centered, self-obsessed society, and the last thing most of us think about is how difficult situations may have happened in the lives of those who have gone before us.

One of the things God is always wanting to do is change the way I ask questions. Instead of asking, "What does this mean about me?" I should ask, "What does this mean about Jesus? And what does it mean about being part of a bigger story than my own, the story of the people of God?"

Maturity happens in the lives of followers of Jesus when they stop looking only to their own preferences and start asking questions about the bigger story of God's kingdom unfolding in the world.

Let's keep it in perspective. Moses faced outlandish challenges—first from Pharaoh, and next from the children of Israel themselves.[8] The disciples where challenged. Have you ever thought about what it was like for the early church? From the time Jesus ascended to heaven, for almost three hundred years the church was severely persecuted, until it became the official religion of the Roman Empire.

When someone says something negative to you on Face-

---

[8]   I just have to say, I totally empathize with Moses. Our family loves to hike, and hiking with three small kids is a tall order. They're everywhere, and before you know it, your leisurely stroll on a beautiful trail is just a stressful chase of trying to make sure your kids don't hurt themselves or anyone else. I can't even imagine wandering in the wilderness for forty years with a million cranky Israelites! I wouldn't blame him if he was like, "Lord, just take me now!"

book because you shared a Bible verse, at least you don't get dipped in wax and lit on fire as early Christians did. The Roman Empire arrested the apostle Peter to crucify him, and all he asked was that they not crucify him in the same manner as Jesus, because he considered himself unworthy. So they crucified him upside down.

Now, I had this really funny experience years ago. In my twenties, my good friend Erika wasn't a Christian, and I had just recently become a follower of Jesus and was constantly bugging her about giving her life to the Lord. Every time we talked, I would make it about Jesus, and she was so annoyed.

One day as she chopped up vegetables for dinner, I sat in her kitchen doing what I always did: bug her about Jesus. And then finally she exploded and said, "You know, I am so sick and tired of it. You're always talking about Jesus. I don't believe in Jesus. I will never be a follower of Jesus. So will you just stop it?" I told her that it was only a matter of time, and she threatened to stab me with her knife.

My face lit up. "Go ahead and stab me. I can't wait to see Jesus!" Erika just shook her head and chuckled.[9]

Poor girl. But I was right. I bugged her right into the kingdom. Two months later, Erika got saved and ended up marrying my wife's brother.[10]

We still laugh about it. I bring this up to illustrate, what's the worst that happens when you talk about Jesus? You get stabbed while someone's cutting up vegetables? Then you get

---

[9] I realize that it was overbearing and a bit over the top. I repent!

[10] I know, it's crazy, but it's true! Erika is my sister in Christ and my sister-in-law.

to go home and be with Jesus. I mean, if you're a follower of Jesus, to live is Christ and to die is gain. And if it's not that bad, you're not doing too bad.

First John 3:13 says, "Do not marvel, my brethren, if the world hates you." That shouldn't be surprising to us. The world hated Jesus. But really, you can find people who hate anything. For instance, I love Twinkies, but I know people who think they're disgusting. How can you hate a Twinkie? All that yellow-cake, sweet-frosting goodness.[11]

In the same way, some people hate certain people, even though God loves them. It's all cray-cray. That's why we have to keep everything in the big-picture perspective of what God is doing in the world, among his people, over the course of history. No matter what goes down, you can rest assured that God is up to something in the world and in your life. And the key to maintaining perspective is our ninth and final fruit of the Spirit: self-control.

Suffering and Self-Control

Self-control allows us to rejoice in suffering.[12] Self-control speaks to power or mastery. It is the ability to control our own countenances and our own hearts in the midst of whatever goes on.

There's an important distinction between self-control and

---

[11] I am amazed that I waited this long to mention Twinkies in this book. And seriously, if you hate Twinkies, you need Jesus . . . *badly.*

[12] Isn't it cool that Jesus placed these qualities *last* in the Beatitudes and fruit of the Spirit? Can you imagine if Jesus put those first? "Oh how happy is the person who gets persecuted. The fruit of the Spirit is self-control." Uh, no thank you! People would have been over it right then and there. And you never would have read this far in this book!

self-mastery (the latter of which you'll find in many popular self-help books). Self-mastery has to do with emotional intelligence and maintaining discipline over your body, mind, and feelings so you can succeed in life and the marketplace. I'm not downplaying the importance of any of those things. Although self-control is not about white-knuckling your life so you can be good—there's a place for that. Take, for example, my friend who had lung issues and wouldn't stop smoking. To some extent, he needed to white-knuckle it and didn't. He needed to put his own desires aside and grit his teeth and stick to creating a new habit of not smoking.

But Jesus isn't talking about good old-fashioned white-knuckling it. See, the self-control that is the fruit of the Spirit is . . . a fruit of the Spirit. Self-control is when the Spirit of God takes the kind of control and influence over your life that, when you stand face to face with temptation, makes you experience the conviction of the Holy Spirit. And then you meet that conviction with repentance and turn and walk away. I love that word *repentance*. Even though it might conjure up images of an angry person yelling at passersby while standing on a milk crate, it speaks of the changes needed to restore a relationship that is in peril.

Self-control is the Spirit of God having the authority in your life to say to you, "There is a more excellent way to live than the way you're wanting to live right now." And when he speaks, you listen and respond.

Self-control is not just you doing a better job, as if it's all up to you. It's all of us as followers of Jesus learning how to surrender our lives more substantially to the work of the Spirit, because he wants to guide us into the beautiful life of faith that's ours in Christ. With self-control, the Spirit of

God influences our decisions so substantially that he gives us back mastery of our lives. But it's really his mastery over our lives in the first place that makes it happen.

And what's amazing is that self-control is built every day at street level. When you're attacked but you start rejoicing and not giving it back in return, as you increasingly groove that into your life, the response of Jesus within you becomes more and more natural to you. Continuing to live out Jesus's beautiful life is both the catalyst for and the result of self-control.

Living out his beautiful life is about our effort . . . and it's not.[13] It's different. It's when we are determined to respond in obedience to Jesus in every moment of our lives. And it's also the Spirit of God harvesting the resurrected life of Jesus in us, working together with us.

And as those things come together—as we live into the blessed life of the Beatitudes and allow the Spirit to bear fruit—then our lives become well pleasing to God. Fragrant. Beautiful.

And as that happens, our lives become crazy happy. Your life, my friend, is a beautiful life in the eyes of God.

When we choose to live into the beauty God created us for and called us to, we end up with the loveliest and maddest cascade of fruitfulness we've ever known: spiritual bankruptcy leads to mourning, which produces meekness. Meekness keeps us hungering and thirsting for God's righteousness, and Jesus promises to satisfy us. Longing for righteousness

---

[13] As Dallas Willard said on page 166 of his book *The Great Omission: Reclaiming Jesus's Essential Teachings on Discipleship* (New York: HarperCollins, 2006), "Grace is not opposed to *effort,* but is opposed to *earning.*" I like that!

causes us to be merciful and pure in heart, seeing the world and other people through Jesus's eyes of compassion. Unfortunately, not everyone wants to make peace, so we end up with injustice and persecution; we get persecuted for speaking up. But that's actually not so bad in the long run, and there are a whole bunch of blessings Jesus promises to those who endure persecution.

And where you live right now—street level in your world—is where this stuff is cultivated. God sent his Son, Jesus, on a rescue mission for you not just so you could say yes to Jesus and keep living how you live but so you might know what it is to live and move and breathe truly beautifully.

Jesus invites each one of us every single day to uncover the treasure, the beauty, that he's folded into us. Studying the Beatitudes and the fruit of the Spirit encourages us because we can see that God has a plan and that it's beautifully woven into every area of our lives. Every single situation becomes an opportunity for us to say, "Lord, not my will but yours be done. Lord, not my life but the resurrected life of Jesus working through me by the Spirit."

And then before you know it, you're so accustomed to saying yes to Jesus and no to the things that used to hold you back that self-control becomes the path to perseverance: the self-control that never stops.

Perseverance enables us to know real godly living as we find our place among the covenant people of God. Among God's family, we find more love than we even know what to do with. And then we're in the perfect position to be vehicles for Jesus's love to enter the world.

11

This Crazy Happy Life

I've heard it said that confession is good for the soul but bad for the reputation. Even so, I want to be a bit vulnerable here with you. Please don't judge me. But the best way to make this point is to trust you with a bit of my brokenness.[1]

Here goes.

I struggle with food.

Don't get me wrong; I absolutely *love* food. No, seriously, I really, really enjoy it. But I have struggled for a long time with my food choices and their consequences.

Being all Italian, there was no way I could grow up not loving food. My mom and my grandma were exquisite cooks. Food was a love language for all of us. If Mom or Grandma loved you, they fed you. If you loved them, you ate everything

---

[1] Plus, if you've made it this far in the book, you realize that God isn't done working on me.

they made you. And you'd better believe you went back for seconds.[2]

My struggles were easy to ignore at first. When I was younger, I had a fast metabolism and played many sports. I could eat anything in sight and stay in decent shape. But such miracles don't last forever. When I hit twenty-five years old, I started to pack on the pounds.

I also found myself leading a more sedentary life. Organized sports ended. I used to joke, "Sure I'm into fitness—*fitness* whole pizza in my mouth!"[3] But the trifecta of poor eating habits, a slowing metabolism, and lack of physical activity took its toll.

Add on top of that that I married Lynn. I don't blame her at all for my struggles. But she loves to serve up big portions. And I love to eat them. Then I gained sympathy weight when we had each of our three kids. If you've never heard of sympathy weight, it is how a dad-to-be can stand in solidarity with his pregnant wife. She grows with the baby, and his belly just grows from food. I love Lynn so much that I couldn't help but grow with her.[4]

Then things got really bad. I remember I wasn't feeling well, and I went to see my doctor. After a physical and some blood work, he called me "Pastor" for the first time. It was

---

[2]   And sometimes thirds and fourths, especially when it was spaghetti and meatballs.

[3]   It is a great joke, but I could literally eat an entire pizza on my own in one sitting (and still have room for cannoli).

[4]   Gosh, I sure hope you are laughing right now. I am chuckling just writing it.

like he was my parents calling me by my full name because I was in trouble. His diagnosis was not pretty. High blood pressure, high cholesterol, excessive weight gain. In other words, *ugh*.

At that point, I knew what I needed to do. I'd gained and lost more than a hundred pounds by that moment. I had been on a few cycles of taking care of myself and getting my health back together. I knew that with regular exercise and healthful food choices, I would be fine. But I couldn't keep it *consistent*. I had the right information, but information was not enough; I needed to *consistently apply* that information to my life daily.

Why did I confess all this to you?

For ten chapters, we've been examining the logic of God's Word: nine beatitudes placed alongside the fruits of the Spirit that go hand in hand. Nine surprising ways that can lead to a truly fulfilling and crazy happy life.

So now what?

I really mean that. *What should we do now?*

In spite of the colloquialism, knowledge isn't inherently powerful. It is helpful as a tool, but on its own, it won't stand up and do anything. It's funny to think about it now, but what I didn't know was that I didn't have any *wisdom* during that particular time of my life when I struggled with food. Sure, I had information, but not wisdom.

I like to say that wisdom is the right application of the right information. Having the knowledge alone doesn't do us much good. We have to let it sink in. We need to encourage it to do its work. We need to let it inform our decisions. When we take the time to give some thought to what God is teaching us, he will help us use it on our journeys. (And I'm not talking about remembering how to tie a bow tie; I'm talking about God using what we've learned to transform us and others through us.)

So I want to give you two things you can do with the knowledge of this crazy happy life.[5]

Be Satisfied

First, you can be satisfied.

You may not remember because it's been a while, but in the first chapter, I claimed that the only reason you and I are so dissatisfied with our lives is that we don't see our lives as beautiful. Every human heart longs for beauty. And that beauty makes us happy.

No matter how tough you are or how ugly your life has been, the longing for beauty is universal. Think about the things people love: art, drama, music, good food, well-made tools and appliances, nature, wide-open spaces, architecture. Those are all glimpses of our deep desire for a more beautiful life.

We hunger for beauty in our relationships. We want harmony, we want a soul mate, we want healthy children, we want . . . *beauty.*

We want to know transcendent meaning and purpose, we want to be connected to something bigger than ourselves, we want . . . *beauty.*

---

[5]   I don't want to limit you either. There are way more than two ways you can act on this information, because God's Word is infinite, like he is. These are just two key things I think are important for walking out a daily life with Jesus and experiencing a life of beauty.

We want beautiful lives.

Dissatisfaction and discontentment are just symptoms of our persistent awareness that our lives aren't beautiful.

But if we know what the beautiful life is in Christ, we *can* be satisfied.

> # Dissatisfaction and discontentment are just symptoms of our persistent awareness that our lives aren't beautiful.

At the end of the day, all the things I just named are simply pacifiers—stand-ins for the real thing—for a deeper longing for this crazy happy life. All our small hungers cry out to the greatest one: our longing for the only one who is truly beautiful, Jesus himself.

As we live out this life we are talking about, we embrace Jesus at a deeper level than we have before. We open ourselves up to real union and communion with him, the one who fulfills every longing of our hearts.

Even though I'm a pastor at an amazing church and I've known Jesus for many years now, I still have to remind myself how we got here, and how we get there.

Stop striving. Don't white-knuckle it. Don't reach down and pull yourself up by your own bootstraps.

Embrace this beautiful life of Jesus, and be faithful about being in his presence and responding to him. Walking step by step with him, you'll find yourself satisfied in ways you never dreamed.

Live a Life That Pleases God

Second, you can live a life well pleasing to God.

We've been talking about it all along—all these different ways we can live in a way that pleases God. But I want to make an important distinction here.

This crazy happy life isn't about trying to please God. As followers of Jesus, we (of course) want to please God. I remember when I was growing up, my sisters and I would be acting absolutely crazy, and my mom would say to us, "You are driving me insane!" And I would sometimes think to myself that we were acting crazy but I'd never actually want to hurt my mom or make her *that* unhappy! Deep down inside, I wanted to please her.

And deep down, we want to please God. But we don't make the choices we make to earn or merit his pleasure. We make the choices we make because we already have God's favor and want to live worthy of our calling. We want to please and not grieve his heart. It's not about earning anything.

This crazy happy life isn't even about us changing ourselves in our own strength. It's not a search for a new or improved self, besides our walks with Jesus.

No, it's about us becoming who we already are in Christ—our truest selves. We are loved. We are embraced. We are accepted. We are redeemed. We are cherished. We are gifted. And we are robed in his righteousness. This crazy happy life, a life that pleases God and is truly fulfilling, is actually who we really are in Christ, as opposed to who we pretend to be or were socialized to be or learned to be over time. This beautiful life is truly who we are.

We lay hold of this crazy happy life in the choices we make

day in and day out, small ones and big ones. So much of life is lived at the moments we decide if we'll follow Jesus or not. When we simply respond, or not.

The process is not usually going to be a cathartic "I'm changing!" kind of moment either. God works in ways that fit into who we are and how he's created us. As we simply respond to Jesus, little by little, layer upon layer, God develops this crazy happy life in and through us.

Remember how I said God's not a God of affirmation but of transformation? Of course, I didn't mean that he doesn't affirm you as a person. He loves you with an everlasting love. But he loves you so much that he won't leave you in the place he finds you. No matter where you are on your faith journey today, whether you've been walking with Jesus for decades or you're just starting out, God wants to do a transformational work in you—right here and right now.

The fruit of the Spirit and the Beatitudes—those nine surprising pairs—make up who you really are in Christ! Every single moment is an invitation for you to say yes to Jesus and simply respond to him so that the fruit of the Spirit of God, who is within you, comes to the surface.

And before you know it, your life is a full-of-happiness, fruitful harvest for God's glory and the blessing of our world. This crazy happy life will also blow your mind and open your heart.

That's the work God is doing today in each one of us who is in Christ. So if you're in Christ, just keep going. Hang in there and abide. Fruit ripens in its own time. Don't lose heart. None of us have arrived; we're just traveling the path together.

And with Jesus, the journey itself is truly beautiful.

I'm learning what it means to be crazy happy in him. It's so much different from what I expected. So much different from all the failed promises of this world. So much better.

Will you join me?

Points to Ponder

Chapter 1
Let's Get Crazy Happy

1. How does Jesus define a beautiful life?

2. How can I experience more of what God has for me?

3. How can I bear more fruit in my life?

Chapter 2
The Crazy Happy Way of Love

1. Where do I struggle to walk in humility?

2. How does Jesus invite me to live with greater humility?

3. How does my pride keep me from truly loving others?

Chapter 3
The Crazy Happy Way of Joy

1. What doesn't break my heart but should?

2. How is the Lord trying to comfort me?

3. What does a life of joy truly look like?

Chapter 4
The Crazy Happy Way of Peace

1. What does meekness really look like?

2. What are my hopes for the future?

3. How can I be a peacemaker?

Chapter 5
The Crazy Happy Way of Patience

1. What does it really mean to desire God?

2. What do I desire that brings me pain?

3. How and where can I trust God more?

Chapter 6
The Crazy Happy Way of Kindness

1. How can I better give mercy?

2. Who do I struggle to be kind to and why?

3. How can I be a kinder person overall?

Chapter 7
The Crazy Happy Way of Goodness

1. Where does God need to purify my heart?

2. How am I struggling to see God in my daily life?

3. How can I walk in goodness?

Chapter 8
The Crazy Happy Way of Faithfulness

1. How can I be a vehicle for God's peace in this world?

2. What other attributes should the church have?

3. What does real faithfulness look like?

Chapter 9

The Crazy Happy Way of Gentleness

1. In what parts of my life do I fear people more than I fear God?

2. In what ways do I silence my Christian witness in order to avoid conflict?

3. How can I be gentler with others?

Chapter 10

The Crazy Happy Way of Self-Control

1. How can I cultivate joy in the midst of suffering?

2. How can I personally work on living with self-control?

3. How does the witness of the church historically encourage me to walk boldly with Jesus?

Chapter 11
This Crazy Happy Life

1.   What do I struggle with?

2.   Where is Jesus seeking to satisfy my deepest longings?

3.   How can my life be more pleasing to God?

Acknowledgments

I am so thankful to Jesus for who he is and everything he has done in my life. I cannot *wait* to see what he does next.

I am also so grateful for the many people he has placed in my life. I want to thank my amazing family: my beloved bride, Lynn, and our great kids, Obadiah, Maranatha, and Annabelle. Next to Jesus, you are the best thing to ever happen to me. I love and cherish you each *sooo* much. And to all the Fuscos, Cappadonas, Dachauers, and all our offshoots, thank you for being our crazy happy family.

I want to thank Crossroads Community Church for being amazing. I am honored and humbled to be part of the Crossroads family. We are learning so many things together as we simply respond to Jesus. Thank you for your grace and patience with me. To pastors Gabe Moreno, Luke Stillinger, and Jason Ritchie, as well as all the Crossroads pastors, staff, and board, thanks for leading with such courage. A special thank-you to my assistant, Diana Blaser, for being awesome at pretty much everything. I couldn't do all this without your help. I also want to thank Bob and Heidi Morter for their dedication in telling everyone that Jesus is real through my nonprofit, Daniel Fusco Ministries.

I want to thank the amazing writing and publishing team I get to be a part of. Lindsey Ponder and Jason Ritchie, thanks for all your hard work and using your amazing writing skills on the manuscript. Alexander Field and the Bindery Agency, I so appreciate your hard work, wisdom, and dedication to help me find the right outlets for my projects.

To everyone at WaterBrook, you have made this such an amazing experience. Andrew Stoddard, thanks for believing in me. Paul Pastor, you are an absolute rock star in general and an amazing editor. Helen Macdonald, thanks for applying your editing skills so adeptly. And to Douglas Mann and Brett Benson and the marketing and publicity teams they work with, thank you for helping launch this book. You are all amazing!

Finally, I want to thank whoever is reading this—yes, *you*. We couldn't do this without you! This is for you . . . because you matter! The Lord sees you and wants to lead you into the crazy happy life. I pray this book helps take you there.

About the Author

Daniel Fusco came to a saving knowledge of Jesus Christ in April 1998, during his last year at Rutgers University in New Brunswick, New Jersey. After a few years as a professional musician (upright and electric bass), he felt called into pastoral ministry. Soon after, he joined the staff of Calvary Chapel Marin, in Novato, California.

After being ordained in 2002, Daniel planted Calvary Chapel New Brunswick. In November 2006, Daniel moved back to the Bay Area and planted Calvary North Bay in Mill Valley. In 2010, while continuing to pastor the church in Mill Valley, Daniel also planted Calvary San Francisco.

In 2012, Daniel turned over both churches to new leadership and moved to Vancouver, Washington. Since April 2013, Daniel has been the lead pastor at Crossroads Community Church, one of the largest and most well-known churches in the Portland, Oregon, metropolitan area. Although churches usually struggle after pastoral transitions, the attendance of Crossroads has almost doubled in size since 2013.

Daniel's teachings have grown in popularity, leading to the formation of Daniel Fusco Ministries. His radio program, *Jesus Is Real Radio,* can be heard across the country, and his TV show, *Real with Daniel Fusco,* can be seen weekly on the Hillsong Channel and other networks. Daniel's *#2Minute-Message* video series on Facebook has grown his page to almost 300,000 followers. These videos are syndicated on Hope with God, a community with over 20 million followers, and Faithwire News, with more than 560,000 followers. You can find his teachings at danielfusco.com, YouTube, and wherever you can download podcasts.

Daniel has written many books and articles. He self-published his first book, *Ahead of the Curve: Preparing the Church for Post-Postmodernism,* in 2007. In April 2016, he released *Honestly: Getting Real About Jesus and our Messy Lives* with NavPress. And in October 2017, *Upward, Inward, Outward: Love God, Love Yourself, Love Others,* also with NavPress. Daniel contributes articles to many major outlets, including *USA Today, Preaching Today,* Pastors.com, *Relevant* magazine, *Leadership* journal, Lightworkers, and Faithwire.

Daniel regularly teaches at churches, conferences, retreats, youth rallies, leadership seminars, seminaries, and college campuses, both in the United States and abroad. His passion for the lost keeps him drinking coffee and playing jazz in and around the great city of Portland, Oregon.

Daniel is married to Lynn, and they have three children: Obadiah, Maranatha, and Annabelle.

To learn more about Daniel, go to danielfusco.com.

Simply Responding to Jesus

At Crossroads Community Church, we are a family of faith, fully engaged, transforming our community and our world.

We would love for you to join us in person at our campus in Vancouver, Washington, or online at **crossroadslive.tv**! Each week, thousands of people from all over the world come together for our live broadcast church services, featuring teaching from Pastor Daniel Fusco and worship with The Responding band. Spend your weekend with us online at **crossroadslive.tv**, **Facebook Live**, and **YouTube Live**, and follow us throughout the week on all social media platforms.

@go2crossroads

crossroadschurch.net | danielfusco.com

Download the Crossroads Mobile App

DANIEL FUSCO
MINISTRIES

At Daniel Fusco Ministries, we're reaching as many people as possible with the message that life is messy, but Jesus is real. Every week, we hear amazing stories of people who have encountered Jesus for the first time through our ministry. Check out the *Real with Daniel Fusco* TV program on the Hillsong Channel and *Jesus Is Real Radio* over the air or on our daily podcasts. Find out more at **danielfusco.com/stations** and **danielfusco.com/radio**.

Do you want to help us reach more people with the life-changing message of the gospel? We invite you to partner with us and join a special group of people devoted to reaching the world at its places of pain. With the love and life-transforming power of Jesus, we can help those who are hurting take the next steps in their journey of faith. Join us at **danielfusco.com/partner**.

 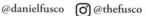